FIND HAPPINESS NOW

How To Get The Relationship You Deserve

Jessie Huff

Table of Contents

Chapter 1: *8 Signs You Were Actually In Love*.................................6

Chapter 2: 6 Tips To Find The One.................................9

Chapter 3: 10 Signs Someone Has A Crush On You.................................12

Chapter 4: 8 Signs A Boy Wants To Kiss You.................................18

Chapter 5: *6 Ways On How To Get Over A Crush*.................................21

Chapter 6: *What To Do When You Have Thoughts of Breaking Up*.................................24

Chapter 7: 6 Dating Red Flags To Avoid.................................27

Chapter 8: 6 Ways To Deal With Gaslighting In A Relationship.................................31

Chapter 9: *6 Signs Your Love Is One Sided*.................................34

Chapter 10: 10 Facts About Attraction.................................38

Chapter 11: *6 Ways To Deal With Betrayal*.................................42

Chapter 12: *10 Ways To Deal With Breakup*.................................45

Chapter 13: *6 Lessons You Can Learn From A Breakup*.................................49

Chapter 14: *10 Signs To Leave A Relationship*.................................52

Chapter 15: 10 Signs You're Dating a Sociopath.................................56

Chapter 16: 10 Thoughts That Can Destroy Relationships.................................61

Chapter 17: *How To Be Your Own Best friend*.................................65

Chapter 18: 10 Signs He Doesn't Like You.................................68

Chapter 19: 6 Signs You May Be Lonely.................................72

Chapter 20: *7 Ways To Deal With An Overly Jealous Partner*.................................76

Chapter 21: **The 10 signs you aren't ready for a relationship**.................................80

Chapter 22: 7 Tips To Get Over Your Ex.................................85

Chapter 23: *6 Ways To Flirt With Someone*.................................89

Chapter 24: 6 Signs You Have Found A Real Friend.................................93

Chapter 25: 6 Signs You Are Emotionally Unavailable.................................96

Chapter 26: 10 Signs You've Outgrown Your Friendship.................................99

Chapter 27: 10 Signs Your Ex Still Loves You.................................103

Chapter 28: *8 Signs Someone Misses You* 107

Chapter 29: 6 Gestures That Make People Feel Loved 110

Chapter 30: 5 Signs Someone Only Likes You As A Friend 113

Chapter 31: *5 Ways To Reject Someone Nicely* 116

Chapter 1:

8 Signs You Were Actually In Love

Falling in love is something some of us might have experienced, but others? They might be new to this feeling, and they might not even know its love. There is no way someone could tell you are in love except for you. Unlike disney princesses, a bird isn't going to come flying and whisper it in your ear. You have to check the facts and feelings in this case. Initially, love will feel very exciting and adventurous, but eventually, you will be settled and calm. Love is a colorful feeling. And here are some ways you can make sure that what you feel towards someone is love.

1. You feel thrilled around them:

When the person you like excites you and makes you feel ecstatic. Then you got it. You are in love with them. But don't be so sure right away; it can be affected by adrenaline rushes in your body. But mostly, it's the feeling of butterflies fluttering in your stomach and doing somersaults. Your excitement is not expected but above average.

2. You want to see them again and again:

Even if they have just left, you always wait to see them again. You wait for the hours where you will see them. If you, by any reason, have to see them daily, then except for getting boring, it gets exciting and interesting day by day. Even though it's not healthy to not let them leave, you must calm down. It is common in love.

3. You always smile around them:

It's hard to stay severe and uptight when someone you love is around. So, whenever they make a conversation with you, you always smile. You visit happily around them, and that makes your mood go up a thousand folds. When you enjoy being around someone, it's natural. Just make sure to keep that jaw in check.

4. You see the good in them:

When we fall in love with someone, all we see is the good in them. Their sound quality becomes the highlight of their personality, and their flaws seem small and irrelevant. You ignore their bad habits because of one good quality they might have because, in love, flaws don't matter. The good always attracts people, and that is what might have tempted you towards them and forward with love with them.

5. Imagining a future with them:

We can't imagine a future with anyone we see and get attracted to. But when you start to imagine a lot with someone, it's apparent that you want to spend it with them. You might want to make them a part of your real life. And it can also happen with a bit of effort and communication. It will work out in the end.

6. You change yourself a little:

Shaping yourself according to someone's need sure sounds unhealthy, but it's a true sign of love. When you do things that they might like and make yourself acknowledged by them, then you want their attention all to yourself. You dress nicely, you put on makeup, and talk more confidently. These are all the basics you do to impress them with your charm and your will to make them fall in love with you.

7. You are overprotected by them:

You have a hawk-like gaze on everyone that watches over your love interest. Especially your same gender. Possessiveness is fine until it becomes extreme. You know all the people who talk to them and ensure that some particular stay away from them. We all understand this level of love, and it is okay to be overprotective of your loved one.

8. You change your priorities:

When you change your sense of style and mindset, it's evident that next in the line is the priority. They come a level higher every time they do the minimum for you. And eventually, you won't even notice, and they are much higher on that list to ignore. That is why keeping them a priority changes many aspects of your life, making you happy for the good.

Conclusion:

Falling in love is harmless and colorful. It's exciting and wholesome. All the words might not be enough to describe it, but it's a good feeling. You have to accept that you are in love with a person and need to do something about it. You need to let them know and believe your feelings, and you never know? They might feel the same.

Chapter 2:

6 Tips To Find The One

Finding someone who matches our criteria can be a difficult task. We always look for a person who is a knight in shining armor. And by time, we make our type. We are finding someone who looks and behaves like our ideal one. We always fantasize about our right one. No matter how hard it may seem to find someone, we should never lose hope. Sharing is always beneficial. And if you trust someone enough to share your life with them, then it's worth the risk to be taken. The person you chose depends upon you only. The advice can only give you an idea, and you have to act on your own.

Now, when looking for someone from scratch can be difficult for many of us. That person can either be the wrong one or the right one. Only time can tell you that. But you both need to grow together to know if you can survive together. And if not, then separation is the only possible way. But if you find the right one, then it will all be good. You have to have faith in yourself. Be your wingman and go after whatever you desire.

1. Be Patient

When looking for someone you want to spend your time with, someone you want to dedicate a part of your life to, you have to devote your time looking for the one. Be patient with everyone you meet so you will get to know them better. They will be more open towards you when you give them time to open. Doing everything fast will leave you confused. Don't only talk with them. Notice their habits, share secrets and trust them. They will be more comfortable around you when they think that you are willing to cooperate.

2. Keep Your Expectations Neutral

When you find someone for you, they can either leave you disappointed or satisfied. That all depends on your expectations. If you wait for prince charming and get a knight, then you will be nothing but uncomfortable with them. Keep them neutral. Try to make sure that you get to know a person before passing your judgment.

3. Introduce Them To Your Friends

The people who love you tend to get along together. The first thing we do after finding a competitor is telling a friend. We usually go for the people our loved one has chosen for us. While finding the one is all you. They can play a part in giving advice, but they can't decide for you. When we see one, we want everyone to get to know them.

4. Don't Be Discouraged

You are 30 and still haven't found anyone worth your time. If so, then don't get discouraged. That love comes to us when we least expect it. You have to keep looking for that one person who will brighten your days and keep you happy. Please don't go looking for it. It will come to you itself and will make you happy.

5. Look Around You

Sometimes our journey of finding the one can be cut short when we see the one by our side—someone who has been our friend or someone who was with us all along. You will feel happier and more comfortable with finding the right person within your friend. It will make things much more manageable. And one day, you will realize that he was the one all this time. Sometimes we can find one in mutual friends. They may be strangers, but you know a little about them already. However, finding the one within your friend can save you a lot of trouble.

6. Keep The Sparks Fresh

Whatever happens, don't let your spark die because it will become the source of your compassion. It will make a path for you to walk on with your ideal one. Keep that passion, that love alive. If there is no spark, then you will live a life without any light. So, make your partner and yourself feel that compassion in your growth.

Conclusion

Finding one can be a difficult job, but once we find them, they can make us the happiest in the world. And if that person is honest with you, then there is nothing more you should need in one. You can always change your partner until you find the one because they are always their ones too. You have to focus on finding your own.

Chapter 3:

10 Signs Someone Has A Crush On You

Have that inkling suspicion that someone likes you but you're not 100% sure about it?

Many of you will agree that there is a certain level of thrill and adrenaline rush when it comes to crushing on someone. It could also lead to feelings of anxiety and nervousness as well.

I'm sure you've been in a similar situation before – where you had a crush on someone and not know how to express or be yourself around that person. But at the same time secretly hoping he or she knows you're attracted to them so that you may begin a romantic relationship with them.

What if you're on the receiving end of that crush, how do you identify the signs and signals that the person is sending you?

Here are 10 Signs that someone has a crush on you:

1.There is a distinct difference in their behavior when they are around you.

It may not be obvious or easily noticeable, but the guy or girl who is secret crushing on you will most likely be nervous when they are around you, or when they engage you in conversation. They might act shy or coy, and maybe even blush when looking at you.

On the flip side, they might also be more enthusiastic in their approach towards you - by expressing cheerfulness because one some level, you make them happy. A person who likes you will pay more attention to the minor details of what you say and what you do. They might also try to make sure you feel great because they want you to feel comfortable and at ease around them as well.

2. They might notice you from a distance.

A person who has a crush on you will likely try to peek a gaze at you from a distance. Whether you are at the same workplace, gym, or friendly hangouts with other friends, if you catch them looking at you more than usual, that is a very big sign that is pointing in your favor. They are also likely to spend a longer time gazing at you or giving you some serious eye contact.

In the digital age, distance could also be in the form of internet presence. They might also try to look you up on your social media channels. A good way to tell is if they start liking your posts and commenting on them. That is their way of entering into your life without being too obvious about it.

3. They will always find excuses to come close or talk.

You can easily understand whether someone is interested in you or not by their enthusiasm for interacting with you. Whether it is trying to match their timings for going to the coffee break with you or adjusting their dates with their friends to take you out to the movie, they will never leave one opportunity to chance to spend that golden time with you. They might also find the silliest of reason for just starting a conversation with you - like asking whether you will teach them something new or bring them somewhere for a meal.

4. Everything you do is appreciated by them.

As a crush, their goal is to make you notice them. To show you that they deserve your attention and time.

If you are going through a bad day, count on your potential crush to talk to you or to make an effort to help you feel better. It is highly likely that your crush will try their best to encourage and make you laugh as well.

They might also laugh at your silliest of jokes. Take it as a form of flattery as it shows that they want to win you over. At the end of the day, as long as it is genuine, it is always better to be around someone who helps you feel good at the end of the day.

5. Lets you know they are always available when you need them.

Another sign that your crush likes you is that they will make themselves available to you as and when you might want to talk. They might be quick to reply your messages when you text them, and they will find time for you whenever they can to engage you in conversations that lets them get to know you more. They might also throw in some hints there to show their interest in you.

6. Makes excuses to touch you!

If someone has a crush on you, they will definitely express interest by engaging in physical contact with you. Be it just as an excuse to feel the soft sweat shirt you are wearing or turning your wrist to appreciate your watch, watch out for these signs. Physical touch is a sign of flirting, and you need to pay attention to them. If they go one step further by poking you or touching you from the back, it is a sure-fire way to know that your someone likes you.

7. Surprise you!

This might not happen with everyone, but there are some people who likes the art of gifting! Especially when they like someone they want to make them feel special, be it bringing them their favorite chocolates and flowers, treating you to a meal, buying you your favorite drink, or getting you something you told them you liked during the last conversation. These are signs that they are paying attention to the little details about you, and that they are trying to express their attraction for you in the form of gift-giving. Friends don't usually buy things for you for no reason at all, so pay attention to this!

8. Borrowing things.

This sign may be rare as well but it could happen. It may sound cliché but when we like someone, we want to keep their things close to us. Any items which belong to you will be special to the person who likes you! Borrowing things could be their way of engaging in interaction with you as well, especially if they are very shy to ask you out.

9. They Compliment your appearance and dressing.

An easy way to know if someone has a crush on you is if they have nice compliments for the clothes you are wearing, for the styling of your hair, or just simply saying you look good today. We say the same when we go on dates to someone we find attractive. We give them compliments to show the other party that we are interested in them. The next time you receive a compliment from someone you suspect has a crush on you, take note of this point.

10. They Ask You Out

If your crush likes you, he or she will most likely ask when you are free to go for a meal or to watch a movie together. They might want to take this time to get you to notice them as more than friends. If they engage in any of the previous 9 signs we have discussed, you could potentially be on a date without even knowing it. So watch out for the signs carefully!.

If however, you are emotionally unavailable, it is perfectly okay to let your crush know at any point that you are not ready for a relationship if you see it being a potential cause of issue for your friendship with them. Ensure that you first confirm that they do indeed have a crush on you before you take any drastic actions to reject them if you are uninterested.

Now that you know what those signs are, you will know how to respond if someone has a crush on you. Do what you will with the information, just do go breaking too many hearts!

Chapter 4:

8 Signs A Boy Wants To Kiss You

You like him, and you're hoping he has the same feelings for you, too. Hanging out with him is such a pleasure, and you always have a great time together. It's easy to tell that he enjoys your company, but how do you know if he only likes you as a friend?

Not knowing whether or not someone you like has feelings for you can be agonizing. One way to know if he likes you as more than just a friend is if he shows some signs he wants to kiss you. You won't need to find the courage to ask him outright. If he wants to kiss you, it will be clear how he feels about you.

Here are 8 ways to tell if a guy wants to kiss you.

1. He's acting flirty

If he usually behaves one way and then all of a sudden seems to act differently (in a smiley, giggly kind of way), then he's flirting with you! His attention is undividedly on you. His eyes are filled with the look of happy mischief because he has kissed you on his mind.

2. He stares at your lips

As you speak to him, he stares at your mouth or keeps glancing down at your lips. He might be doing it deliberately, hoping that you'll get the hint that he wants to plant one on you. Or, he might not even know that he's doing it. But because he's thinking about kissing you, his focus will keep going to your lips.

3. He makes a comment about your lips or mouth

He might also comment on your lips, such as, "you've got the cutest lips" or "what's the color of this lipstick you're wearing?" this is one of the sure signs a guy wants to kiss you. He definitely likes you and is going to make his move soon.

4. Lingering eye contact

He doesn't just look at you, but he gazes into your eyes. If the guy you like starts looking at you the same way you look at a chocolate-covered donut (if you're into that sort of thing), then you can be positive that he likes you as more than just a friend.

5. He makes physical contact

If he's planning on kissing you, he might break the ice by touching you a little in subtle ways. A stroke of your arm, a hand on the cheek, and even a one-armed side hug are all ways he will get you used to make contact with him before he gets even closer.

6. He seems a little nervous

He might normally be confident around you, but if he starts acting nervous, clumsy, or distracted, it may be one of the signs he wants to kiss you. He might have a feeling that you like him, but his not knowing for sure might make him afraid of your reaction when he does try to kiss you. So don't be surprised if he seems to have lost his confidence all of a sudden.

7. He falls silent suddenly

Falling silent is a similar sign of nervousness before an impending kiss. He's probably busy thinking about how, where, or when he's going to make his move. He might be thinking, "is this the perfect moment for our first kiss?"

Building up the courage to finally show a girl how you feel can be scary. It's no wonder he's lost in his thoughts.

8. His voice softens

Psychologists say that when a guy starts using a softer tone of voice, it is one sign that he wants to kiss you. For some reason, whispered voices go along with passion and proximity. I mean, speaking loudly or abruptly isn't sexy, is it? So it makes sense.

If his tone of voice changes, know that he's attracted to you and wants to kiss you.

Knowing if a guy has feelings for you might not always be easy. But if he does want to change the status of your friendship, one of the ways you'll know for sure is if he shows signs he wants to kiss you. So, if you notice any of the signs described above, all you have to do is be prepared for your first kiss and your new romance.

Chapter 5:

6 Ways On How To Get Over A Crush

At the time, having a crush might feel like the best feeling in the whole world. It makes you feel mature and young at the same time. When we see someone we like and get butterflies fluttering in our stomach, that is not without any reason. It might be because you have a crush on them. It can either be a slight go-to crush. The one where you like the person and get over them as soon as you find someone new. Or a big crush on someone, where you get stuck on a person for a reasonable amount of time. Usually, it's tough to get over a crush.

No matter how ecstatic someone would feel while crushing on someone, we someday have to get over it. It's a healthy way to lead a life. A crush should have to be gotten over within time. That feeling of wondrousness is limited and has to go someday. It may take a lot of time to get over it. But with the right amount of work and the right amount of feelings, we can get over a crush with no difficulty. Listed below are some ways to get over a crush.

1. Welcome Your Emotions

When you have a crush on someone, the best thing you can do to make things easier is accept these feelings and emotions. Telling yourself constantly that you don't like them will only add up to your problems. Accept the fact that you want someone and have a crush on them. It's pretty standard for a person to have a crush on someone. So, naturally, it's normal for you too. It will help you move on from them much easier if you have already accepted the feelings about them.

2. Take Your Time

You can't overcome a crush in one day. Even though it takes work and confusing emotions, it also takes a lot of time. Be patient while getting over an infatuation. If it is just a crush, then you will someday get over it. Don't rush things, and it will only confuse you with your feelings and get mixed signals from you. It will just be a matter of a week or month. Then you will be fresh and happy again.

3. Busy Yourself

When you sit by yourself all day, your mind will automatically go towards thinking about your crush. You will get the time to fantasize about them. This way, it will be much harder to get over someone. It would be best to keep yourself busy in your daily routine to avoid letting your feelings consume you. When you don't get the time to think about them, you will eventually get habitual of not remembering them daily. And slowly, you won't even notice, and you will completely forget them.

4. Talk With A Friend

Talking with someone familiar with the situation and someone who you trust fully can help a lot. A friend is needed in this situation sometimes. You can always talk to them about getting over your crush. They will help you get over them and will also help you go through the emotional pain. It's common to have mixed and confusing emotions at this time, so talking with someone who has a clear mind will let you understand the circumstances.

5. Try Meeting With New People

The easiest way to get over a crush is by meeting new people. Try to meet someone who might replace that crush for good. They might make you feel good about letting go of that part of your life gladly, as a desire can be pretty brutal. It would be best to make sure that the new person in you is there for a genuine relationship and not only to serve a purpose.

6. Know Your Worth

Running after someone who doesn't even return your feelings is not worth your time and energy. When you know that you deserve better than this, you will eventually get over a crush. They won't even have the idea of the struggle you put up to meet them. They will take you just as another person in their life. So, be it. Identify your worth and get over it.

Conclusion:

Getting over a crush can be pretty tricky for us, but we need to get over them at the right time. Don't work yourself out while doing so. It's normal to have a crush, and you will have much more in the future too. Just don't let it consume you.

Chapter 6:

What To Do When You Have Thoughts of Breaking Up

It's not always easy deciding if you should break up with your partner: You probably care about them and have many great memories together. But there could be real issues in the relationship that make you wonder if it's best to end things. Whatever outcome you settle on, however, it's a good idea to first ask yourself a few questions so you can be sure it's the right decision for you.

"Breaking up with your partner is the best thing to do if you feel like you're not happy anymore, and the relationship is just pulling you down instead of pushing you up.

Here are some things to think about before ending your relationship, according to experts.

1.Is There Anyone Influencing My Decision?

If you're seriously considering breaking up with your partner, it's wise to take a moment to think about what — or, more specifically, who — might be influencing you toward this decision. Is your mom insisting you'd be better off without them? Does your best friend swear that splitting up is your best option? Although people's opinions can be a good guiding force, at the end of the day, this is your choice, not theirs.

2. Do We Hold the Same Core Values?

When you and your partner first got together, you might have initially bonded because you have similar interests. But if you're now at a place where you're thinking of taking the next steps or breaking up, it's worth asking yourself if the two of you align on values, too. "Preferences in daily life will change, but core values will likely not change. "You could feel like it is time to break up with your partner because those [incompatible] core values are showing themselves."

3. Would I Want My Child to Be With Someone Like My Partner?

It may seem like a strange thing to consider if starting a family isn't on the horizon, but it can be an effective litmus test to picture how you'd feel if your child were with someone like your partner. "This will trigger a reality check — would you want your children to spend the rest of their lives with the same kind of person as your partner? "If your answer is no, then take it as a sign that you are heading in the right direction ending the relationship."

4. Is This A Pattern for Me?

Are you someone who starts thinking of breaking up with your partner a few months in each time you're in a relationship? Do you start losing interest at about the one-year mark? Ask yourself whether this is a genuine impulse or if it's just a pattern for you. "Is the reason I desire to break up with someone unique to this person, or would it apply to multiple people?" Clara Artschwager, "If it applies to more than one person, this is often indicative of a larger limiting pattern in relationships."

Are you scared of getting too close to someone? Are you afraid of commitment? Reflecting on these things can help with your decision.

Chapter 7:

6 Dating Red Flags To Avoid

When dating someone, there always stands a risk. A risk of not being happy or a threat of choosing the wrong person. That is why elders taught us to make smart decisions smartly. But what can one do when it comes to finding the one. Acknowledging a person you want to date won't be enough. Many factors revolve around dating. That is why it is essential to recognize red flags in your relationship. So, we should never hurry to commit to someone. Take your time. There is a lot more than getting to know this person. When initially dating, we always need to make sure to know where our comfort zone lies.

Red flags are the danger signs of a relationship. It can save you a lot of time and positivity. And it's not necessarily true that only the other person is to blame. Sometimes we fail to give them our part of affection, and gradually it becomes a disaster. Even if we overlook the minor toxicity, ignoring the major red flags is not suitable for you. Don't hesitate to give your opinion.

1. Shortfall Of Trust

The one major thing we all need to date someone is trust. Doubt will only make things difficult for you and your partner. Trusting each other is vital in a relationship. And when you date someone, trust grows slowly. And if your growth is based on lies and cheating, then that trust is as thin as thread. You can't force yourself to trust them either. If it doesn't come naturally, count it as a significant red flag because trust is the first thing that comes when dating someone.

2. Change In Personality

In a relationship, we have often seen people change their personalities around different people. If the same is happening to you, then you have to be careful. If they act differently around you, it indicates that they are not themselves in front of you. That is one major red flag in dating that shouldn't be ignored. They try to act the way you would like, instead of the course you are in. And eventually, they will get frustrated. So, it's better to be yourself around everyone. That way, your relationship will be genuine, and you feel a lot happier.

3. Toxicity

An abusive relationship is the worst kind. When someone is not attentive towards you or shouts at you constantly, you become the submissive one. It would be best if you took a stand for yourself equally. Most of the time, people stay quiet in times like these. But it's to be known that it is a dangerous sign in your dating life. It's a red flag that needs to be taken into notice. You don't have to cope with them; leave them be. Find someone who matches your energy. A toxic person is just as bad as drugs. We need to be careful around them.

4. Feeling Insecure

Sometimes, a relationship that is not meant to be, leaves you feeling insecure about yourself. You constantly question your place in that relationship. Where do you stand in their life? It leaves you thinking about all the flaws you have and examining all the wrong decisions. You have to know that it works both ways. And whoever they are, they have to accept you no matter what. You start to contribute more than your partner when it should be all about equality.

5. Not Being Around Each Other

When we dive into a relationship, we feel the need to be comforted. And when the person opposite you makes you feel uncomfortable, it's a major red flag in your dating life. You both need to make sure to be there for support. If not, then that relationship doesn't hold any significant meaning. If we do not feel secure or satisfied, then what do we get from this relationship? Because that is the most important thing that we might need from someone. But it's essential to play your part as well. Both sides should give their all for their dating to work.

6. Keeps Secrest From You

What someone needs in a relationship is to share their lives. Talking is the basis of communication that builds a relationship. But if your partner keeps secrets, then how can you grow together? You always need to speak for better understanding and comfort with each other. If they are acting fishy, you can't spy on them. It's a red flag that you need to catch.

Conclusion

You need someone who provides you with what you deserve. If you feel someone is not suitable for you, then feel free to break up with them. It would help if you were your priority. And make sure others know how important you are to yourself and should be important to them too.

Chapter 8:

6 Ways To Deal With Gaslighting In A Relationship

We call it gas lighting when someone manipulates you into thinking that you are confused about your feelings or when someone makes you doubt them. It is crucial to know if you are gaslit in a relationship to break that chain of toxicity. It leaves you with doubts as well as insecurities within yourself. So good to end it as soon as possible. People gaslight others to make sure that you do what they want. You will notice that gradually you do things that they would like you to do. They manipulate you into doing what they like.

People who gaslight others' in a relationship trivialize their feelings. They will address your even tiniest of feelings as overreacting. They try to control the situation their way. Changing details about something that happened in the past and constantly blames you for everything they did. When it comes to your needs or wants, they frequently change the subject, ensuring that you always think about what they would like or want. They keep you low on the priority list while they keep themselves upon yours. All we need is to be safe from these kinds of people. For that, the following are the ways to deal with gaslighting.

1. Confirm Manipulation

People may confuse someone's rude behavior or childish behavior with gaslighting. It's not always necessarily true that the other person is gaslighting. It might be their true nature to talk with an attitude. It is commonly mistaken for gaslighting in a relationship. Gaslighting is the repetitive behavior of deceiving or manipulation the same person. If the person is not polite towards you, then it may not be considered manipulation in any way. People may gaslight you unintentionally too. When they say something in the heat of the moment, it doesn't necessarily mean they want to manipulate you.

2. Speak Up

When you stay quiet in times of raising your voice, then it becomes a habit. When they know that you won't speak up to them about their behavior, they burden you more. You get habitual of not speaking back, and they get habitual of getting away with manipulation or lies every time. Show them that you won't accept the way they treat you. They will eventually find their mistake or find out that it was not worth it.

3. Stay Self-Assured

When a manipulative person tries to change the small details about any event, you need to be confident in your version of the story you think happened. When they see you constantly hesitating, then they become more confident in their version. They will start making you doubt yourself in a way that whatever they say sounds true. You need to be firm on your point and make them see that you know the truth of the situation.

4. Self-Aid

No matter what you think is vital in your life, it would be best if you were your priority, always. Self-aid or self-care is extremely important for a person to follow with or without a relationship. A gaslighting person will always try to make themselves your priority. In that case, you need to stand your ground and show them that you come first in every aspect of your life. With self-care, you will be active mentally and physically. You will get the power to fight for yourself.

5. Communicate With Friends

It's more reliable to talk to others about your situation. When you are confused about your partner's behavior, you can always ask for support from someone you trust. They will help you get a better idea of the situation you are in and maybe help you get out of it. Third-party who knows both sides of the story will help you sort out your relationship.

6. Administrative Support

It is always helpful to seek professional knowledge from people as they know much better than us and understand the situation much more clearly. Ask them for help. They will professionally help you out and make sure you are okay. Gaslighting is not to be taken lightly. Professional service will always be available for those who feel like reaching out for it. There is no embarrassment in seeking executive help.

Conclusion:

There are lots of people who are suffering from gaslighting. If you think that you are one of them, then you need to follow each step carefully. Make sure that you feel safe and sound in your life. The person gaslighting will eventually make their mistake but don't wait for them too. Get out of that toxic relationship as soon as possible.

Chapter 9:

6 Signs Your Love Is One Sided

While some things are better one-sided, like your favorite ice-cream cone that you don't want to share, your high school diary that knows all your enemies and crushes, and a game of solitaire. But a healthy relationship? Now that should be a two-sided situation. Unfortunately, when you're stuck in a one-sided relationship, it becomes easy to fool yourself every day that what you are experiencing is normal, when in reality, it could actually be toxic or even unworthy and loveless.

They could physically be sitting next to you, but you will find yourself being alone because of your emotional needs not being taken care of. Even though you have committed yourself to your partner, there's a fundamental difference between being selfless in love and giving it all without receiving anything at all. It might be possible that you're in denial, but the below signs of your one-sided love are hard to ignore.

1. You're Constantly Second-Guessing Yourself

If you don't get enough reassurance from your partner and constantly wonder if you are pretty enough, or intelligent enough, or funny enough, and always trying to live up to your partner's expectations, then you're definitely in a one-sided relationship. You tend to focus all of your energy and attention on being liked instead of being your true self and nurtured by your partner. It would be best if you always were your authentic self so the people who genuinely deserve you can get attracted to you and get relationships that match the true you.

2. You Apologize More Than Needed

Everyone makes mistakes. We are not some divine creatures who are all perfect and have no flaws. Sometimes you're at fault, sometimes your partner is. But if you end up saying sorry every single time, even if you had no idea about the fight, then maybe take a deeper look at your relationship. You may think that you're saving your relationship by doing this, but trust me, this is a very unhealthy sign. Cori Dixon-Fyle, founder and psychotherapist at Thriving Path, says, "Avoiding conflict results in dismissing your feelings." Solving fights should always be a team approach and not just one person's responsibility.

3. You're Always Making Excuses For Your Partner

Playing defense is excellent, but only on a soccer team. Suppose you are doing it constantly for your partner and justifying their behaviors to your circle of friends, family, and work colleagues. In that case, you're overlooking something that they are most likely seeing. If the people in your life are constantly alarming you, then maybe you should focus on your partner and see where the signs are coming from.

4. You Feel Insecure About Your Relationship

If you are never indeed at ease with your partner and often question the status of your relationship, then it's a clear sign that you are in a one-sided relationship. If you focus more on analyzing yourself, becoming more alluring, and choosing words or outfits that will keep your partner desiring you, then it's a major red flag. To feel unsettled and all-consumed in a relationship is not only exhausting, but it's also sustainable. Feeling constantly depleted in your relationship is also a sign that it's one-sided.

5. You're Giving Too Much

Giving too much and expecting just a little can never work in the long run. Suppose you're the only one in the relationship who makes all the plans. Do all the chores, remember all the important dates and events, consider stopping or making your partner realize that they aren't giving much in the relationship. Often when people give, they have some expectations in the back of their mind that the giving will be returned, but things fall apart when the other person never had those intentions. It's normal for a short while for one partner to carry the load more than the other; all relationships go through such stages, but constantly engaging in it is unhealthy.

6. You're Never Sure About How They Are Feeling

You can't read people's minds, nor are the communications transparent; you may end up overthinking their behaviors towards you and may be confused about how they're truly feeling. This uncertainty would cause you to dismiss your feelings in favor of thinking about them. This connection may be filled with guessing and speculations rather than knowing reality and seeing where they genuinely stand.

Conclusion

The best way to fix a one-sided relationship is to step away and focus on your self-worth and self-growth instead of trying to water a dead plant. You must focus on flourishing your own life instead of shifting your all to your partner. Your mental health should be your priority.

Chapter 10:

10 Facts About Attraction

Everything from taking an interest in someone to admire someone physically or mentally is known as an attraction. The attraction could be a romantic or sexual feeling. Attraction can be confusing and takes time to understand. Most of us find it hard to know what we feel about or are attracted to someone. We couldn't figure out what type of attraction it is, but we should remember there is no right way to feel the attraction. There are so many types of attraction, and some could happen at once.

1. Women attracted to older men:

So, it is expected that most women these days are attracted to older men just because of their "daddy issues" and the most one is the financial issue but according to study it's not the reason. According to authentic references or studies, the women born to old fathers are attracted to older men, and the women born to younger men are attracted to younger men. As they think that they will treat them just like their father did.

2. Opposite attraction:

As we all heard before, "opposite attracts." well, it is true, according to a study of the university of dresden, that both men and women are attracted to different leukocyte antigens, which is also known as the hla complex. A genetic blueprint responsible for the immune function is so unique that this attraction has to do with species' survival. Now, how do our brains detect the opposite hla complex? According to a study, our brain can see the opposite hla complex only by the scents; isn't it a fascinating fact?

3. The tone of women's voices:

According to a study by the university of canada, when women flirt, their voice pitch increases automatically. Not only while flirting, but women's voice tones increase at different emotions. The highest tone of a woman's voice gets when she is fertile or ovulated, and guess what? According to studies, men like the most high-pitched voices of women.

4. Whisper in the left ear:

According to a study, when you want to intimate someone, like whispering " i love you" in their ear, then whisper in their left ear because whispering in the left ear has 6% more effect than a whisper in the right one.

5. Red dress:

Red dress attracts both men and women. It is examined in a study that usually men love women in the red dress. They find it intimidating.

6. Men with beard:

Women find men attractive with a beard. Beard with the subtle cut. Another fantastic fact about the beard is that women judged men with a beard to be a better choice for a long-term relationship. This might be because men with beards look more mature and responsible. Beard also makes you look like you have a higher status in society.

7. Men trying to sound sexy:

So, women have no trouble whatsoever changing their voice, but men have no clue about it. Women lower their voice pitch and make it sexy, and men find it so attractive, but men find it very difficult to sound sexy. It got a little bit worse when men tried to say sexy. The reason behind this is elaborated in research, according to which men are not focused on making their voice sexy but women do.

8. Competing:

Research shows that when you are famous for everyone, and everyone likes them, you get attracted to them and try to get them. You start competing for that person with other people, which makes you feel more attracted to that person. That person will be in your head all the time because you see everyone admiring and chasing that person.

9. Adrenaline:

Studies show that adrenaline has to do a lot with attraction. People find others more attractive when they are on an adrenaline rush themselves. According to a study, women find men more attractive when they are ovulating than in another period.

10. Weights and heights:

When taking a liking to someone. People always prefer to choose a person who holds the right weight and height according to them. Different people may have different opinions. When they find a person with a likable body, they get easily attracted to them.

Conclusion:

Attraction to someone can play a significant role in getting them. When people are attracted to you, they make you feel worth it all, and you feel ecstatic. Attraction can be=ring in a lot of factors like popularity, relationship and of course, love.

Chapter 11:

6 Ways To Deal With Betrayal

Betrayal is a strong word. And the most challenging part of it is recovery. Healing from something someone has done to you that you were not in favor of can be as hard as counting the number of hair on your head. The first thing that comes in our way is our emotions. Anger, rage, and regret. But, what can one do to save themselves from such a move? They can only be careful with the people around them. Trust issues have always been challenging to deal with. And betrayal only fuels that fire. We often turn to others for support, and sometimes they turn out to be deceivers. It may leave us unprotected.

No doubt that betrayal changes someone to some extinct. The person may feel insecurities within themselves. They start to doubt and stress themselves. It often leads to self-harm, too, at times. And the most severe of them all would be anxiety. Because no matter what, we can't ignore the fact that someone has lied to us and made us believe them. Betrayal is painful. And it's common to have experienced it once in your life. When someone you trusted with your secrets or emotions has broken that trust, that feeling of not being valued enough makes us hate that person, whether they did it intentionally or unintentionally. But there can be some ways to deal with betrayal.

1. Take Time For Emotional Improvement

After a heartbreak, what we need is time. Time to think, time to process, and time to heal. We can't instantly forget about anything that has happened to us. "Time heals all wounds." And that is precisely what we should do. Take a break. Try to do things you want. Make yourself feel light and collected. Stay away from the person who hurt you. This way, it will help you bury that memory quickly. Try to think about it as little as possible. Make sure you have other things on your mind instead. Rearrange your priorities from the start. This time you believe in yourself more than you felt in that person.

2. Overcome Self-Hatred

It is often that you would feel hatred towards yourself. Because you sometimes believe that it was your fault, to begin with. The thing with betrayal is that it is one-sided. The other person can do nothing but suffer. Naturally, you would be pitying yourself for their actions and feeling insecure. But it's not worth your time or emotion. You need to get a hold of yourself and talk some sense into yourself.

3. Try To Forgive and Forget

We all know that it is not as easy as it sounds, but it is more beneficial. When someone betrays us, we feel the need to take revenge. Hurt them the way they hurt us. But nothing can be as comforting as forgetting it ever happened. We all will remember a part of it, but it doesn't have to come between your life. It takes a lot of determination to forgive someone you don't want to ignore, but you will see the pros of it in the future. If you decide you take revenge, then it will leave you guilty and regretful in the future.

4. Ask For Help From The Trusted

It may be difficult for you to trust anyone after being betrayed. But you can always go to someone for comfort. If a possible third party can support you, don't hesitate to reach out to them. Make sure you talk about it with someone so you can take advice and feel light. It will help you to deal with the situation quickly. It will give you the peace of mind that will help you all along the journey ahead. It is recommended to talk with someone who had a betrayal in their life.

5. Acknowledge, Don't React

There is a significant difference between responding and reacting. We should be in control of our emotions. We need to acknowledge our feelings. After betrayal, our senses are more likely to be mixed up, leaving us confused. But that is a recipe for disaster. It will only be harmful to you to react without analyzing the situation appropriately. You can't ignore the fact that you have been hurt, but you will feel calmer by the time.

6. Be Careful Next Time

No one can ensure that we won't get hurt again. But we can be careful around people. That doesn't necessarily mean having trust issues with people but detecting the people who can hurt you. And with each time, you will get better and better at dealing with betrayal. It would help if you felt those emotions to overcome them every single time. And after each series of betrayals, you will become stronger than before.

Conclusion

Betrayal can be heart-wrenching, but it should not stop you from being happy in life. Cry and grieve for a day or two. And then get up again as a stronger person. Believe in yourself. Let go of the past and focus on your future, for it can bring much more happiness.

Chapter 12:

10 Ways To Deal With Breakup

Even if your relationship wasn't going well and the thread was on the edge of breaking, ending it all can be very hard and hurtful. It can be even more hard when you gave it all and thought that things were going smoothly from your side, but your partner disagreed and wanted to cut everything off. Wallowing in grief can be a normal phase after a breakup, but it's high time that you get over it and come back to normalcy. Here are some ways you can deal with breakup.

1. Remove them from all social sites:

If you're thinking of going on a complete social media fast after your breakup, it might be a good thing for you. But if not, consider removing them from all of your social media. Even if the split was amicable, seeing them might renew a twinge of sadness in your heart. You don't want to see their new love interest or how they're enjoying their lives without you.

2. Reconsider staying friends:

As much as your heart and brain try to convince you to stay friends with them after breaking it off, it's always a bad idea. Maybe you both can be friends later on, but immediately? A big no! It will be way more hurtful and awkward to see them every day and share a bond as friends only when you both know that bond was much stronger before. Seeing each other will only make it worse for both of you to move on.

3. Call some friends:

The worst thing you can do to yourself after a breakup is isolating yourself from the world. This would lead to you overthinking about your mistakes and would lead to bad decisions. It would cripple your mental health, and you will find yourself in a never-ending guilt loop. Instead, call your friends, hang out with them, talk to them and cry to them. Laughing with your friends is the best therapy that you can easily afford. You will feel much better with having someone around.

4. Stop blaming yourself:

Get yourself out of the mentality of "i could've done this instead" or "i could've done that instead." if the relationship was bound to fall off, there was absolutely nothing you could have done or said that would have saved it. A relationship always requires the efforts of two; if you have put enough measures or didn't put much, then the two of you weren't a good fit.

5. Take a break:

If the relationship was all mushy and long-term, or you had a messy breakup, now will be the perfect time to take some break from dating. As much as you would feel pressured and in need of starting something new soon, you might be carrying a lot of unattended emotional baggage that you need to settle down before taking a step ahead.

6. Don't dwell on fixing the relationship:

It is just so much you can do to save the relationship. And once it's gone, consider it gone. Scheming and plotting on getting back with your ex would ruin your mental health. Instead, try to start focusing on yourself and your mental health. Improve your lifestyle and let bygones be bygones.

7. Eat healthily and exercise:

Binge eating in this time of sadness is fine if it's short-term. But if you keep nibbling on junk food, it'll ruin your physical health as much as your mental health. Not having proper nutrition will leave you more stressed out as you won't be having the essentials to deal with stress. Abandon your sadness and indulge in eating healthy, and work out more to gain mental peace.

8. Get enough sleep:

If you force yourself to stay up late at night, anxiety or sadness may overwhelm you and keep you from sleeping. It would be best if you had a proper sleep to keep yourself functional and stable. Pen down any negative thoughts you have and let them flow away from your body to the paper.

9. Neither ignore nor wallow in your feelings:

Ignoring your feelings will eventually cause an emotional outburst that you might not even be ready for, whereas wallowing in your emotions will cause you to revisit all your memories and subconsciously hurt yourself. Instead, you must healthily deal with your feelings and move on.

10. Stop obsessing:

It's natural to keep thinking about your relationship and obsessing over it after your breakup. But after a while, you should jerk the thoughts off whenever they intrude on you. It would be best to direct yourself towards more positive and constructive ideas and healthily get over your breakup.

Conclusion:

Getting over a breakup isn't easy at all. But if you prioritize yourself and your needs, you will be there more quickly than you might know.

Chapter 13:

6 Lessons You Can Learn From A Breakup

Have you ever been in a relationship, and it hasn't ended well? Breakups may make you feel insecure about yourself; if your significant other has broken up with you, you might feel rejected. Although watching tv shows and eating a tub of ice cream may sound like the only logical thing to do after a breakup, it is the time to focus on yourself and see what went wrong in your previous relationship. Relationships teach us who exactly we are, it tells us what kind of people we want to love. Here are a few lessons you can learn from a breakup.

1. Happiness Comes From Within

At the start of a relationship, we all feel excited and beyond happy, but happiness is not true happiness. Happiness comes from within. This means that we don't want to have anyone else in our life to feel happy. Sure, you would feel lonely after a breakup, but time heals everything. When you are with someone who doesn't treat you the way you should be treated, then you might've forgotten your self-worth. You need to remember that you were not born with this person; this relationship was just a part of your life. You need to start loving yourself, start accepting that this is the way you are. Once you start believing that only you can make yourself truly happy, you will finally understand the true meaning of happiness.

2. It's About Us

Breakup helps you to understand that it was never about them; it was always about you. When going through a breakup, people often blame everything on their significant other, but it is not always about them. Breakup gives you space for your personal growth. A breakup is very enlightening, although it may bring out some insecurities but as soon as you tackle your inner demons, you realize that it is all about you.

3. You Can't Change Anyone

Haven't we all heard someone saying that we will change them? It may sound effortless trying to change someone's habits, but it is pretty impossible in reality. We cannot change someone unless that person also wants to change. Change comes from within, and not even your love can change your partner. If you and your partner broke up, it probably was for the best even though opposites attract, but too many differences can cause many problems. It is time to accept the fact that you need to find someone who satisfies your needs.

4. Believe In Your Gut

When something isn't right or the way it should be, we all feel about it; it can be our instincts warning us. Listen to your gut. Often, we tend to ignore what our gut is telling us, and we carry on like everything is fine when it is the opposite. Sometimes, your gut tells you that this is not the one, but ignoring it will lead to a bad breakup. So always listen to what your gut has to say; it's just your heart telling you what it wants.

5. Figure Out What Your Heart Truly Wants

When we go through a breakup, we all know it happened for a reason; there was something about that relationship that you didn't want. Now is the time to figure out what you want from a relationship. It is the time to focus on yourself, understand your emotional needs, and how you want a relationship to be. It is time to figure out what kind of a relationship you want. Once you figure this out, you know what you do and what you don't want from a relationship.

6. It Is Okay To Be Alone

After a breakup, some people feel abandoned as if they are all alone now, and they feel like it is not a good thing, but in reality, it is okay to be alone; you don't always need to be with someone. When you realize that you can make yourself happy and you don't want anyone else to do that, it is the time when you need to become selfish and think about yourself. Set some goals, achieve them, and don't just throw yourself into another relationship without figuring out what you truly want because it may just end up in heartbreak.

Conclusion

Breakups are hard to go through, but they happen for a reason; try to figure out what indeed went wrong. What you want from a relationship and remember it is okay to be alone; you don't need someone else to make you feel happy. You are enough for yourself.

Chapter 14:

10 Signs To Leave A Relationship

According to a tinder survey, around 40% of millennials won't stay with the wrong person just for the sake of keeping their long-term relationship. Sometimes it's better to let go of the person you've been dating for a long time if you notice that your relationship doesn't make you happy or, even worse, makes you feel uncomfortable and depressed.

A study suggests that certain signs can tell you it's time to leave your partner. And while they don't always mean all is lost and there's no point in fighting for your love, they could help you figure out if there's a problem.

1. You keep breaking up and getting back together

According to research, on average, more than 1/4 of couples will break up and get back together at some point. And this might even end up becoming a never-ending cycle of on-again-off-again relationships. Maybe you're second-guessing yourself and decide to give your partner a second chance, or you're afraid to let go and move on. But it's important to break that cycle because this kind of relationship might not do you or your partner any good.

2. You don't like yourself

Not liking yourself in a relationship can be exhausting, especially if you don't like who you've become because of your partner. Maybe you've distanced yourself from your family that you love or feel less motivated to try to achieve your goals because of them. If your partner is constantly bringing you down in any way, instead of inspiring and being supportive, it's time to cut them out of your life.

3. Your partner is constantly criticizing you

It's one thing to mention what you don't like about how your partner behaves, which can be a healthy thing to do and help you better communicate with each other and improve yourself. But it's a different thing when your partner criticizes your personality and character.

4. You're afraid of being alone

Fear of being single is not a good enough reason to stay in a relationship, especially if there're signs that your partner isn't right for you and you're not happy. Studies have shown that people who are afraid of being single settle for any partner just for the sake of being in a relationship, no matter how this affects its quality. However, that doesn't make the situation any better, and that fear will also make it harder to get out of an unsatisfying relationship.

5. You live in the past

If you think about how much fun you used to have with your partner and how happy you were with them in the past more than you enjoy the actual relationship in the present, this is a red flag. Being more in love with the memory of who your partner was or what your relationship used to be like won't bring you happiness once you realize that this is the only thing keeping you from leaving. So it's important to distinguish between what's gone and not coming back and what's real and worth staying for.

6. Your partner is too unpredictable and intense

Some people can be nice and charming one moment and then suddenly angry the next. This behavior can make you feel scared and intimidated, and you always need to walk on eggshells around them to prevent triggering them, even in little ways. That means your partner is emotionally volatile.

7. Your relationship is superficial

When you've just met someone, it's understandable that you won't immediately open up to them and reveal your deepest secrets. Your conversations will be focused on more simple things, like your hobbies or your job. But with time, it's natural for you and your partner to grow close, which means you aren't afraid to show your more vulnerable side and discuss more serious topics.

8. Your relationship is one-sided

If your partner only wants to be with you when they need you, for example, when they had a bad day at work or some other problems, this is not a good sign. They might be using you to get attention while not caring about what you need. And if you constantly do all the work in your relationship, supporting your partner when they don't do the same for you, you might be stuck in a toxic relationship.

9. Your partner often says he'll leave you

If your partner threatens to leave you, for example during fights, or when they can't make you do what they want, this might be a form of psychological manipulation. They're using your fear of abandonment to control you. This controlling behavior might extend to different areas of your life, so it's important to recognize it and put a stop to it before you get hurt.

10. You don't want to share good news with your partner

If something positive has happened in your life, but it doesn't even cross your mind anymore to share it with your partner, it might be a sign that your relationship is in trouble. This might mean that you feel like your happiness is irrelevant to your partner because they don't care about you as much as they used to. And if that's true, and they don't genuinely encourage you and feel happy when you succeed, it might be time to leave.

Do you recognize these signs from your previous relationships? How did you decide that it was time to break up?

Chapter 15:

10 Signs You're Dating a Sociopath

Opening

Before discussing the signs that you're dating a Sociopath or not let's first understand the term sociopath. It'll make things even more digestible for you.

Currently, around 1 % of the US population is suffering from the personality disorders of Sociopathy. A sociopath disregards people, society, and important societal rules around them. They are extremely self-assured and think about being more talented and better looking than others. Think about Hannibal Lecter, Joker, Patrick Bateman, John Doe, the Buffalo Bill, and many others on the list. Are you a true devotee of Hollywood? Then visualize Charles Manson, Ted Bundy, and Jeffrey Dahmer in your mind. Yes, these are the most precise and realistic character roles of Sociopaths.

According to Dr. Scott A. Bond, Sociopathy is a learned behavior that is often the result of some form of childhood trauma.

Main

In today's video, we will be taking a closer look at the central signs to spot a sociopath so that you can make an informed decision on whether to leave the relationship or to stick it out despite knowing the risks.

1. They get Jealous

Mostly sociopaths get jealous of their partner and blame them for everything. You might find yourself defending against the continuous false accusations of your partner. They would never encourage you to pursue your dreams or achieve anything because of their never-ending jealousy.

2. They Lie about Everything

Lying is never okay under any circumstances; however, Sociopaths lie with every breath. They do it on a regular basis and without any regrets. They find themselves smart doing this because they figure that you might not even know. While trust should be the foundation of any relationship, Sociopaths seemingly lie to their partner with perfection and they are good at planning and telling a foolproof lie which can be difficult to even guess.

3. They are always Arrogant

They constantly consider that they are better than other people are. They are constant swaggers and like boasting about their running speed, nice clothes, or shoes. This attitude in the relationship could be extremely negative, abusive, and uncomfortable. You need to watch out if your partner is always invalidating you and bragging about their capabilities.

There is a possibility that they feel superior in every way and there is no one else that can match the same skill-set they own. If you tell them about their mistakes they will be annoyed and their arrogance in such situations will touch the skies. They might even feel portray that you have hurt their self-respect.

4. They don't think about Consequences

It is often exciting for people to engage in impulsive behavior sometimes, but sociopaths tend to participate in impulsive activities regularly. Apart from being dangerous, it can result in dealing with adverse financial consequences. The same goes in the decision-making process of a relationship. If your partner does not think about the negative consequences of their decision, then you might be dating a sociopath.

5. They don't want to Change

While most people learn from the mistakes and consequences of their poor actions, sociopaths don't pay attention to any of this. These people show zero desire to learn from their mistakes and bring positive change in their attitudes. Their consistently disregarding attitude will make it extremely challenging. Watch out for this sign.

6. They do not tag along with Rules

You may think that it can be exciting to break some rules in the beginning with your date, but if it is a regular occurrence, there may be something wrong there especially if it is an act that concerns criminal behavior. Be mindful that this can ruin your present and future. Watch out if your partner engages in reckless behaviors that are out of the norm and don't hesitate to bring it up with your closest friends and family if you find something amiss.

7. They do not Care

Yes, it is normal to have some days off, but you need to watch out if your partner never cares about anything. A healthy relationship is based upon mutual give and take. If your partner never empathizes with you, then the possibility is that you are in a relationship with someone who might only care about themselves. Since mutual care and kindness are the essences of a healthy relationship, these warning signs should ring some alarm bells for you that you may want to consider walking away from this relationship.

8. They are the Loners

Their antisocial personality makes it extremely difficult to make or maintain a close relationship with others. A sociopath shows extremely antisocial behavior with others and does not seem to have any desire to make any friends.

9. They Relentlessly Ruin Things

A sociopath prioritizes his or her needs over their partner and continuously looks for excitement above all else. They ruin everything with no one left to clean up the mess. If you are regularly facing financial crises left behind by your partner, then you might be dating a sociopath.

10. They have Impulsive Mood Swings

A characteristic trait of a sociopath is that they tend to have unstable or unexpected mood swings, expressing abrupt temperamental changes when things are not going their way. If you said something unexpected and your partner responds with controlling and manipulative behaviors, be careful as this could be another tell-tale sign.

Closing

If any of the above points rang any alarm bells in you, it is time to start paying close attention to these details. Start asking yourself the right questions. While you may have the inclination to give your partner the benefit of the doubt, never become too complacent and assume that you need to stay with someone who doesn't treat you like you rightfully deserve. If you believe that your partner is a sociopath, seek help, talk to a counsellor, your family member, or your close friends. They might be able to paint a clearer picture for you to make an informed decision on the next best move for you.

So, that's it for today's video. Did we miss out on any elements of a sociopath? Let us know in the comments section below. Do not forget to subscribe to our channel, like, and share this video.

Thank you!

Chapter 16:

10 Thoughts That Can Destroy Relationships

You might enjoy the beauty and joy that comes with being in a loving and committed relationship, but it's not always butterflies and beds of roses. It's ubiquitous for you or your partner to transform your insecurities into fears and negative thoughts, but they don't treat you right; they may take a toll on your relationship. Negative thoughts may turn into negative actions, which can lead to unhealthy communication, and could impact how you start seeing your significant other. If you relate to any of the below thoughts, it might be time to reevaluate your relationship and how you view the situation.

1. They don't love me anymore:

Although it's pretty common to worry about whether the sparks of love are still alive in your partner's heart or not, constantly asking them whether they still love you might do more harm than good. It could stir up a lot of conflicts based on your insecurities and fears. Even if your partner reassures you by šaying that they love you, it could put them in doubt as to there must be a matter causing these concerns. Instead of swinging and jumping to conclusions, communicate effectively with your partner in a way that's suitable for both of you.

2. The power word "should":

It is more or less a major red flag to not tell your partner about what you're thinking rather than automatically assuming that they should know how to read your mind. Blaming your partner for understanding the things that are affecting you secretly, like, "he should know how much it bothers me when he doesn't give me time" or "she should understand how busy i am these days" isn't fair at all. You should be able to voice all your frustrations but in a way that you make your partner understand and not push them away.

3. The blame game:

It's easier to point fingers at your partner and blame them for your spoiled mood rather than taking actions against yourself. Blaming them only postpones any improvements that are needed in your relationship. Instead, try talking to them about it. Tell them when they are wrong and apologize for something that you did to hurt them. We can never predict or control others' emotions, but we can very well hold our own.

4. Overactive imagination:

This mostly happens when you're overthinking about a situation and jump straight to conclusions without having any actual evidence. For instance, if your partner is coming home late at night and they're telling you it's because of the heavy workload, you automatically assume it's because they're having an affair and they're lying to you. These may happen when you have a piece of unattended emotional baggage from previous relationships. It's important to understand that you know your partner well, and they will never do such a thing to hurt you. Have a conversation with your partner about this and seek reassurance if needed.

5. Comparing and contrasting:

You start to put your partner under the pressure of unrealistic expectations when you compare them with a person you see as ideal. For example, if you met your best friend's boyfriend and witnessed an action they did, and you wished that your boyfriend should do the same, you might be disrespecting your partner by asking them to change into who they aren't. It's unhealthy to put that sort of pressure on them. Instead, ask your partner politely if they're willing to do that for you since you liked a particular quality or trait in a person, but you should also tell them that they are lovable regardless.

6. Fantasizing:

Unless you are in a toxic relationship, reminiscing and fantasizing about someone other than your partner might badly affect your relationship. It's because you will keep thinking about the possibilities of being with someone else rather than working on the flaws of your relationship. This might destroy your relationship in ways you can't even imagine.

7. All or nothing:

Seeing your partner as a perfect human being without mistakes, flaws, or imperfections is an idea for destruction. Having extreme thoughts that they can do no wrong or thinking that they always do the wrong thing can mess up with your own and your partner's mental health. Try accepting their failures and mistakes, and keep in mind that, like you, they're just ordinary human beings.

8. Label slinging:

Constantly putting labels on your partner, like calling them lazy when they couldn't complete their chores or calling them insensitive if they don't address a particular issue, may cause problems in your relationship. Instead, we should try to see the positive things in them and help them improve themselves.

9. You think you can't compete with their ex:

Their ex is their ex for a reason. Constantly trying to be like them and asking about them isn't helpful in any way; it can make your relationship weak and your partner frustrated.

10. You think that you're hard to love:

Worrying about pushing your partner away while addressing your insecurities is normal, but that doesn't in any way mean that you're hard to love. Everyone is special and unique in their tracks and can be loved by their partner no matter what.

Conclusion:

While these thoughts might be the perfect recipe to destroy your relationship, a little effort, and hard work into it can go a long way and save your relationship.

Chapter 17:

How To Be Your Own Best friend

Why would you want to become your own best friend? There are several benefits to creating your internal support system rather than relying on your partner, friends, or family to be there for you when you're suffering. Having other people's expectations can lead to disappointment, heartbreak, and relationship breakdown if your expectations aren't met. We all have it in us to give ourselves what we need without seeking it externally.

Of course, it's great if you have a strong support network, but you could still benefit from becoming more self-reliant. And what about if you have no one to turn to for help, or if your current support people are unable to be there for you?

Isn't it far better to know how to support yourself in times of need? Here's how to become your own best friend.

1. Be Nice To Yourself

The first step to becoming a friend is to treat yourself like you would treat a friend. That means that you need to stop being self-critical and beating yourself up. Start by acknowledging your good qualities, talents, and abilities and begin to appreciate your unique self.

When you catch yourself thinking up some nasty self-talk, stop and ask, "Would I say this to my best friend?" If not, then reframe your self-talk to be more supportive and caring.

2. Imagine How You Would Support A Friend In The Same Situation

Think about a loved one, a friend, a family member, someone dear to you and imagine that they are in the same situation you are currently facing. Think about how they're struggling, suffering, and feeling stuck with this problem, then consider how to best offer assistance and advice to them.

Craft the words that you would say to your greatest friend and then say them gently to yourself. Allow yourself to feel supported, and give yourself what you need.

3. Honor Your Needs

Following the theme of considering how you would help a dear friend, **you need to start taking your advice and putting your own needs first**. Do you need a day off from work? A long hot bath? An early night? A wild night? Some time to catch up on your reading, cleaning, gardening, creative projects, social life, or self-care?

Whatever you need, allow yourself to **put it at the top of the list rather than the bottom**. Be there for yourself and make it happen.

4. Send Compassion To The Part of You That is Hurting

Being a friend to yourself involves adopting and mastering the art of self-compassion. Compassion isn't forceful or solution-focused. **Compassion is accepting, peaceful, and loving, without the need to control or change anything**.

Imagine a mother holding a child who has bumped his head. Her compassion is a strong force. She simply holds her child with loving, comforting, gentle arms and whispers, "It will be alright, my love." The child trusts his mother's words just as you learn to trust your own words when speaking to yourself.

Imagine yourself as both the child and the mother simultaneously. Offer compassion at the same time as you open up to receive it.

Use these techniques to become your own best friend and start *being there* **for yourself!**

Chapter 18:

10 Signs He Doesn't Like You

Is your man as invested in you as you are with him, or does he simply not like you? If you're struggling to decide whether or not he's into you, here are 10 unfortunate signs that he probably doesn't like you.

1. You have to initiate all of the conversations

If you only talk to this guy when you make an effort to send him a text, email, or pick up the phone and call him, he might not be that into you. Professional matchmaker kimia mansoor says that when a guy is smitten, he'll want to learn as much as possible about you. Yes, he may be nervous and intimidated by you because he likes you, so you'll make want to make sure that isn't the case first. But if you are making all the effort and he's not even responding, let alone starting the conversations, it might be time to move on.

2. He doesn't protect you

A surefire sign that he doesn't like you is if he doesn't protect you against the big and little things in life. Does he make sure you're safe when you cross a busy road? Stick up for you in a verbal argument with someone else? Or put his arm around you when you're feeling vulnerable? There are many ways for a man to protect his girlfriend or wife. The key thing is that he should want to do this because it's built into a man's dna to seek out relationships that allow them to feel like a protector.

3. You notice him flirting with other women in front of you

If your guy hasn't let go of his flirtatious behavior after dating you a few times, it could be that he's not invested in the relationship the way you are. This likely bothers you more than you are letting on, so be honest with yourself about whether or not you think it's okay for him to do that and then make a decision about whether or not to carry on in the relationship.

4. He doesn't seem to care if you flirt with other men

In retaliation for his flirtatious behavior, you start to flirt with other guys, and your man doesn't even seem to care. It could be that he's comfortable with your relationship and trusts you not to cheat, but it's more likely that he doesn't care what you are doing because he's not interested in making this relationship stick. If he's not getting jealous, perhaps he doesn't care enough.

5. He doesn't ask you to hangout

You always have to ask him to do stuff like going to the movies or out to dinner. If every date is your idea and your man doesn't offer any suggestions to hang out or even watch television together on a saturday night, he's already checked out. He might be a relaxed type of guy that doesn't like to initiate, but most likely, he just isn't invested enough to make a time commitment. It's time to move on and give him an ultimatum. Don't waste your time trying to get him to hang out. He might be a relaxed type of guy that doesn't like to initiate, but most likely, he just isn't invested enough to make a time commitment.

6. He's all over the place emotionally

If your guy seems to be hot for you one minute and then ice cold the next, you might be wondering what's going on. Maybe he is not fully over his ex. You're not alone: it's hard for girls to read guys whose emotions are unpredictable. If your guy is not showing up for you consistently, you're probably tempted to find one who can.

7. You can feel like he's not listening

When you are together – which isn't very often – you feel like he's on another planet or has his face buried in his phone. Is he listening? Who knows! But if you feel like he's not, you are probably right. You can try testing him to see if he is, but more often than not, you'll find yourself frustrated with his lack of interest in your conversations.

8. You have no idea who his friends are

A guy who has no interest in continuing a relationship won't invite you to meet his friends. If it's been any length of time and you've heard all about his buddies, but he's never introduced you, be aware: he might not want them to meet you.

9. You can only hang out when it works for him

When you set up a date, he never makes concessions to make time for you and always puts his job, friends, and family first. While that seems noble and loyal at first glance, it's pretty annoying after a while, and you might start to feel like you are not a priority for him in his life. If it is only one time, that's acceptable, but that could become a problem if it is a regular pattern.

1. You don't think he's trying hard to get your attention

Guys like it when girls pay attention to them. If your guy isn't making a fool of himself somehow, at least some of the time to try to get your attention, it might be that he doesn't care if he has it. It's hard to hear, but guys have telltale signs of being into a girl. Wanting to be close and trying to get your attention is always at the top of that list.

Chapter 19:

6 Signs You May Be Lonely

What is that one emotion that leads us to anxiety, depression, or stress? People often feel this emotion when they have no one around to support them. That is being lonely. What is being lonely? "When one is unable to find life's meaning," or simply put, it is the feeling of isolation. You often find yourself in a corner then outside with friends or family. Sometimes, these emotions are triggered by discouragement by close ones and negativity of life. We try to bear it alone rather than risking the judgment of others. We try to hide it as much as possible. Then, eventually, it becomes a habit. Then even if it's news worth sharing, we keep it to ourselves.

Loneliness can drive a person to harm themselves, either physically or mentally, or both too. It can change our lives drastically. Going out seems to be a burden. It feels tiresome even to move an inch. So, we tend to stay in one place, probably alone. But it doesn't always mean that you are feeling sad. Sometimes you feel happy being alone. It all depends on how you look at things.

1. Feeling Insecure

When we look around us, we see people every day. This type of connection with people can lead to two conclusions. Positive or negative. A positive attitude may lead to appreciation. However, negative emotions will lead to insecurities. This insecurity will lead us to go out as little as possible. And whatever we hate about us, we feel it more prominent. Eventually, we never go out at all. Because of the fear that people might judge us at our worst trait. We think that even our family is against us, which makes it even more difficult.

2. Anger Becomes A Comrade

It becomes hard to express what we feel to others. When we feel like there is no one we can genuinely tell our feeling to, they bottle up. We start to bottle up our emotions to don't get a chance to tell others about them. And those bottle-up emotions turn into anger the most easily. Even the slightest thing could make us aggressive. We get angry over all petty stuff, and gradually, it becomes our release to all the emotion. It becomes easier to show your anger than other emotions.

3. It Starts To Hurt Us Physically

Stress is one of the feelings you get out of being lonely. It is only natural that you stress about everything when you are alone in a situation. Scientifically, it is proven that staying alone most of the time raises our stress hormone, and it becomes a heart problem in the future. Most of us have experienced the tightening of our chest at times. That is when our stress hormone raises it builds up around our heart. It may also result in inflammation and some vascular problems. So, being lonely all the time may be physically harmful to us, and we should take it seriously.

4. Highly Harmful To Mental Health

Mental health is just as important as physical health. We need to focus on both equally. Loneliness can be harmful to our mental health in many ways. It often leads to hallucinations. It causes depression and anxiety. These types of mental occurrences are proven fatal if not dealt with immediately. It also drives us to overthink, which is equally as harmful as others. Isolation keeps your brain in a constant phase of resentment.

5. Lack Of Hope and Self-Compassion

Getting lonely sometimes is okay. It gets serious when you do not want to let go of it. When there is no hope, it feels like there is no reason to return—staying alone forces you into feeling empty and unwanted, thus, losing hope of ever being wanted again. Because discouragement surrounds us, we feel safe staying alone most of the time. We lose all the passion we once had, and it makes us dull. Things that once we loved doing feel like a burden. Gradually, we become addicted.

6. Negativity

Positivity and negativity are two aspects of daily life. And in life, when loneliness is our companion, we choose negativity to go through our day. Everything seems to be too much work, and everything in life seems dark. Negativity is the only thing we keep because it looks more suitable to lonely people. It causes emotional harm to people and tends to get in the way of an average daily routine. However, the negative side is what we choose every day.

Conclusion

We can feel lonely even after being surrounded by people because it's just something people feel in themselves. They don't realize that there are people who are willing to talk to them. Being lonely can cause one a lot of harm and disrupt all the day's work. But it doesn't always mean that lonely people are unhappy. Loneliness can bring peace too.

Chapter 20:

7 Ways To Deal With An Overly Jealous Partner

Being jealous in a relationship seems cute at first, but it can really kill the love you and your partner have for each other after a while. You'll probably start to see the negative aspects of over jealousy pretty clearly. Some people have bad experiences and trust issues due to their past relationships, so being in a relationship with a jealous person shouldn't necessarily be a deal-breaker. It can be started by finding why your partner is feeling the way they feel, especially when you haven't given them a reason to mistrust you in the first place.

If your partner is being aggressive and trying to control what you're doing, you might want to try to work together with them to fix the issue. It will give them the reassurance they need and create a closer bond between you two. If your partner is turning red with jealousy lately, here are some signs for you to deal with them.

1. Talk About Their Fears and Anxieties

It would be best to calmly sit your partner down with you and ask them what's going on in their mind if you feel like your partner's jealousy is getting off the hook. Make sure you're listening to them fully attentively, and don't be scared to express how their thoughts affect you. Danielle B. Grossman, a California licensed marriage and family therapist, says, "Do not try to minimize, negate or 'fix' the fears. Do not try to bully your partner's fear into submission. Do not belittle, humiliate, shame, and threaten the fear." Always be empathetic and give them your undivided attention. Make sure you never attack your partner and make them trust that they can confide in you.

2. Don't Get Defensive About Your Behavior

If your partner is accusing you of something that is far from true, do not feed the fire by jumping right away into an argument. Evaluate the situation first. If you instantly try to get defensive, your partner will misinterpret your reaction or may get even angrier. Try to be patient first and deal with the situation calmly. Reassure them that whatever they're thinking isn't right, and you're always going to be with them no matter what.

3. Be Extra Affectionate

After discussing the reasons for their jealousy, show your partner extra love, during this weak and vulnerable time. This is the time to be more generous with your affection. Try to touch them more, make small gestures for them, and be supportive throughout this time. Of course, this means that you should take the abuse if extremely unhealthy jealousy is present. Don't let them force you into situations that you are uncomfortable dealing with.

4. Create Boundaries

Setting boundaries in your relationship isn't a negative thing at all. Loads of people in healthy relationships create a line to understand each other's emotions and priorities better. People should be aware of their selves even within a relationship. According to a Ph.D. psychologist Leslie Becker-Phelps, "You need to know what you like and dislike, what you're comfortable with versus what scares you, and how you want to be treated in the given situations." So, try your best not to let your mental health affect by your partner's conflicts.

5. Be Available and Responsive:

Although this issue is something that your partner needs to fix on their own, it can still help the situation get better if you're responsive when they reach out to you. If you're there when your partner needs you the most, and you tend to comfort them, it can help calm their jealous habits. This takes a lot of effort, without a doubt, but if your partner notices that you're available and receptive, then the trust between you two will only grow stronger with time.

6. Revisit The Issue and Be Patient

Over jealousy is an issue that can't be fixed overnight. You must be patient with your partner and show them now and then that you're willing to work on this problem together by supporting and discussing their fears. It can indeed be time-consuming and emotionally draining, but don't let it stop you from trying to work things out with your partner. Take baby steps, celebrate small victories until it isn't an issue anymore.

7. **Rebuild Your Trust**

If your partner is losing trust in you, make sure you gain it back by doing small things, such as facetiming them and texting them throughout the day, explaining to them why you're running late, or taking a rain check in advance if you know you're busy that day. Reassure them with positive statements, and this will eventually put your partner's fears at ease.

Conclusion

There's no magic spell or easy way to deal with a jealous partner, but if you want to make the relationship work, then put effort into it. Get your partner to trust you, be empathetic with them and talk about their feelings. This little bump in the road can probably go away, which will help you in the long run.

Chapter 21:

The 10 signs you aren't ready for a relationship.

Relationships can be complicated sometimes, but what makes them more complicated is we ourselves. There are times when we fail to understand when to step back and think in a different way about life. We often fail to understand where we stand and where the relationship should stand leading to a lot of anxiety and pain in the long run. Sometimes it's more important to step out of the flow and give yourself time to think about things deeper.

Here are 10 signs that show you might not be ready for a relationship just yet at this very moment:

1. When you aren't happy with your own self.

We often feel a relationship or another person can make us happy, but unfortunately, unless you are happy with your own self, no one can come and make you happy. As the saying goes, happiness is within. It is very important to first find what makes you happy in life and gives you freedom. Because unless we know how to make ourselves happy, we cannot be at peace with another person too.

2. When you feel a relationship will help you overcome your loneliness.

We all do get lonely sometimes. But a relationship isn't the solution for overcoming that. When we expect another person to help us get past the loneliness it just creates a lot of pressure on the other person and might end up suffocating them too. Read a good book, make some nice dinner, watch that favorite rom-com alone, get that pet which you always wanted, because you need to be your best friend first and when you know how to overcome your loneliness, the other person will love your company too.

3. When you aren't sure about the person and jumped into the relationship faster than you wanted to.

As much as it is important for someone to understand themselves, it is also very important for us to know the person we are planning on getting in a relationship with. Do you see that person with you 10 years down the lane? Is he the one you had dreamt your life with? A relationship is a two-way street. It is very important to express and set your standards and expectations in the relationship clear.

4. When you still aren't healed from your past.

We all have a past. Some memories are good some still give us nightmares, but it is very important to consider it as just a life lesson and move on. The more we stick to our past, the more distant we get from our future dreams and goals. If you keep thinking about how your ex broke the promises and cheated on you, you won't be able to see the good intentions of the current person who probably could have been there in the future too, but you couldn't be completely happy with them based on your past instincts.

5. When you have fear of commitments and the idea of making sacrifices pushes you away.

We all have fears inside of us. Fear of how things will turn out in the future, we get apprehensive of taking a serious step in life. Commitment should be given only when you are ready from inside because for any relationship to work out both of you should be on the same page and only when your heart tells you are ready!

6. When you have a lot of insecurities and self-doubts.

No one likes to stay with a person who is full of self-doubts and always needs validation for everything in life. You need to be confident about your own self first because only then you can grow in the relationship and motivate the other person to grow too. Too many insecurities come in when there is not enough communication and when you cannot openly express your fears to the person.

7. When the relationship is not motivating you to grow into a better version of yourself and boosting your personal growth.

If you find yourself in a relationship where your personal life and growth are stagnant, then you are with the wrong person. As much as you should be investing in the other person it is also very important to invest in yourself and help the other person invest in themselves too. If the relationship doesn't motivate you to achieve that dream, get that dream house one day, travel together to the favorite destination, have that dream cruise, and get the dream car together, then you might as well feel the need to rethink why is it so.

8. When you feel situations are one-sided in the relationship.

Sometimes we end up with people who are not as much into us as we are into them. Their efforts and actions don't match their words. So it is very important to be vocal about your expectations in the relationship and not stay in one just for the sake of being in a relationship. Along with love, understanding the sentiments, emotions, and vulnerabilities of a person is also very important and if the person is not matching up to the mark, life is too short to give chances to a person who won't care as much as you would.

9. When you get hindered in communicating openly.

Open communication is very important for a healthy relationship. If you are having inhibitions about talking about your problems and insecurities to the person, either because you feel they won't understand you or because any discussion with the person ends up in an argument, then quite understandably you are with the wrong person and need to get yourself out of the relationship.

10. Peer pressure and wrong decisions.

This happens for marriages too. Any kind of relationship should not happen under pressure. If it's because all your friends are engaged and/or committed to someone, doesn't necessarily mean you have to do the same. There are many more things to experience in life. Unless you really want to get along with someone, you shouldn't go in it just because you feel cornered and lonely among your friends. Make better choices and better stories to tell them and make them feel jealous of your single but happy life! ;)

Chapter 22:

7 Tips To Get Over Your Ex

When you get together with someone, it feels like that relationship will never come to an end, but sometimes things just do not work out the way we wanted them to. Break-ups and ending all contact is probably one of the hardest things to do. Sometimes, you start obsessing over them, over the life they might be leading without you. But one thing a person should remember after a bad break-up is that you weren't born with that person; you have lived without them and can do the same again; it just needs a bit of work and time. Here are several ways to get over your ex.

1. Social Media Detox

The most common way of communication is now social media, but we all know its disadvantages. It has made it hard for people to move on; seeing your ex again and again in pictures on social media may provoke some unwanted feelings. So the best way to not feel that way is to get off of social media for a while or unfollow your ex; commit yourself not to check their page or the page where there is a chance you might see them. You just need to gather some willpower and try not to stalk them, which will quickly help you move on.

2.   Let Go Of The Memories

When you first start dating someone, it feels right and like you are living in a fantasy. The beginning of a relationship brings many expectations along with it; there are things you expect from your partner and something that your partner expects from you. But when these expectations are crushed, one may feel hurt. A person starts to miss someone when they remember the great times together, so you need to remember that you broke up for a reason. Try to remember what your ex did or didn't do that lead to this break-up. There is always a reason behind a break-up, so place the causes, and you will find yourself realizing that it ended for a good reason.

3.   Get Rid Of The Things That Remind You Of Your Ex

In a relationship, we all receive gifts and heartwarming cards and letters, which may make you feel happy at that time, but after a break-up, these cards and gifts may serve as a reminder of your ex and bring back some unwanted but sweet memories. These precious memories can lead you to believe that you miss them. So as soon as you break up with someone, get rid of their reminders. This can include small gifts, cards, clothing because these can lead to obsession.

4.   Love Yourself

Loving yourself sounds like a total cliché, but you can never move on from someone without loving yourself. When someone dumps you, you might feel lowly about yourself, and the self-worth you had in mind may get dropped. As much as it sounds easy, it is not. True happiness and love need to come from within. You need to start appreciating yourself, connect with yourself again, and you will start feeling that you don't want anybody else's love to survive because your own is enough.

5. Visualise Your Future Without Them

In a relationship, people make plans and set goals together. So when you break up, you might feel confused as to what to do next, as all your dreams of the future include them. When trying to move on, remember you had a life before them, a life with goals to be achieved. Visualize your future without them; try to set some goals for yourself. Think about all the things you can do now that you couldn't have done with your ex. Visualizing your future without them will help you accept that this relationship is over. You may have a lot of options now that you no longer feel tied to someone. You can set your priorities again.

6. Don't Contact Your Ex

You can set a few rules for yourself when you break up with someone, and these rules should include a no-contact rule at least until you've moved on. Do not contact your ex until you have moved on and accepted everything. Hearing their voice can bring back a lot of memories that will not let you move on.

7. Move Or Redecorate

If you used to share your living space with your ex, literally everything in your house will remind you of them. Move out if you can, but if moving out is not an option, you can redecorate the home, change the furniture positions, and buy some new accessories for the house. Redecorating the house is an activity that you may feel excited about, buy the things you have always wanted but couldn't because of your ex.

Conclusion

Bad break-ups can mess someone up but fortunately, working on yourself can help you move on, so remember that you are a complete person without them, and you don't need them to live your life.

Chapter 23:

6 Ways To Flirt With Someone

No matter how confident and bold we assume ourselves to be, we tend to freeze up and utter a wimpy 'hey' when we see our crush approaching us. Flirting doesn't always come easily to everyone, and there's always struggle, awkwardness, and shyness that follows. But, some people are natural-born flirters and just get the dating thing right.

Knowing how to flirt and actually showing someone that you're interested in them sexually or romantically can be a minefield. But once you get your hands on it, you'll probably become an expert in no time. If you struggle with flirting, we've got some tips to help you master the art of flirting and getting your crush's attention. Below are some ways to flirt with someone successfully.

Be Confident But Mysterious

There's nothing sexier than someone who has a lot of confidence. Of course, I'm not talking about being too overconfident, and it will tend to push people away from you. But if you're strutting down the halls as you own them, your crush (and everyone else) will notice you. Don't give away too much of yourself while being confident. People tend to get intrigued by someone who gives off mysterious vibes. They show their interest in you and avail every opportunity to try to get to know you better. This will lead to you having a chance to make up a good conversation with your crush and even flirt with them in between.

Show That You're Interested In Their Life

Who doesn't love compliments and talking about themselves all the time? We come along with people who mostly like to talk than to listen. If you get a chance to talk to your crush, don't waste it. Ask them questions about their life, get to know their views and ideas about certain things like politics, fashion, controversies, show that you're genuinely interested in them. They will love your curious nature and would definitely look forward to having another conversation with you. This will also give your brownie points of getting to know them better.

Greet Them Whenever You Pass Them

Seeing your crush approach you or simply seeing them standing in the halls can be the scariest feeling ever. You will probably follow your gut reaction and become nervous; either you'll walk past them hurriedly or look down at your phone and pretend like you're in the middle of a text conversation battle. But you have to ignore those instincts, and you have to look up at them and simply smile. You don't have to indulge yourself in an extensive conversation with them. Just taking a second to wave or say hi can be more than enough to get yourself on your crush's radar, as you will come off as polite to them.

Make Ever-So-Slight Contact

The sexiest touches are often those electric ones that come unexpectedly, not the intentional ones that might make someone uncomfortable.

Unnecessary touches can be a turn-on because they signal a willingness to venture beyond the safe boundaries that we usually maintain between ourselves and others. But be careful not to barge into them accidentally. Small, barely-there touches that only the two of you notice are the best. Let your foot slightly touch theirs or lightly brush past them.

Compliment Them

While everyone loves receiving compliments, try not to go overboard, or they would be more likely to squirm in their seat rather than ask you out. You should compliment them lightly about their outfit or fragrance or their features or personality, but keep the subtle flirtation for when the time and moment is right. Giving them compliments would make them think that you're interested in them and want to step up the equation with them.

Look At Them

Experts suggest that we look and then look away three times to get someone's attention. According to the Social Issues Research Centre, maintaining too much eye contact while flirting is people's most common mistake. Our eyes make a zigzag motion when we meet someone new - we look at them from eye to eye and then the nose. With friends, we look below their eye level to include the nose and mouth. The subtle flirt then widens that triangle to incorporate parts of the body. Please don't stare at someone too intensely, or else you'll end up making them feel uncomfortable.

Conclusion

It might seem nerve-wracking to put yourself out there and start flirting, but fear not! It's normal to get nervous around someone whom you like. Follow the above ways to seem confident and pull off a successful flirtation. Know the importance of keeping a balance between revealing your feelings and keeping the person you like intrigued.

Chapter 24:

6 Signs You Have Found A Real Friend

Life seems easy when we have someone by our side. Everyone makes at least one friend in their life as if it comes naturally. That one person who we can rely on in difficult times. That one person who cares for us when we forget to care for ourselves. Friends are family that we get to choose ourselves. So, we have to decide that person exceptionally carefully. Friends are people who know who you are. You can share both joy and sadness with them without hesitating.

Friends have a significant impact on our lives. They can change us completely and help us shape ourselves into someone better. However, there might be some forgery in your way. Some people consider themselves as your friend, but we fail to notice that it is otherwise. So, it is imperative to choose a friend carefully, while an essential fraction is dependent on our friendship with someone. A good friend is the one whom you can count on to hold you when you require one. A friend is someone who becomes selfless when it comes to us. They always stay by your side as it said, "friends till the end."

1. You Can Be Yourself Around Them

No matter how you behave in front of your family or co-workers, you can always act like yourself in front of your friend. When they give you a sense of comfort, you automatically become yourself. That is the reason you never get tired of a friend. Because who gets tired of being who they are. A friend is a person who accepts us with all our flaws and stays by us even in our worst phase. They find beauty in your imperfections. That type of friend becomes necessary to keep around.

2. A Support For Good And Bad Times

We all are aware that support is what we want in our time of need. To share our difficult times and to share our good news with someone. A friend listens. They listen to whatever you want to ramble to them without complaining. They understand you and try to give to advice as well as possible. They are an excellent shoulder to cry on. They feel joy in your happiness. They feel sadness in your loss. Friends are people who love us, and thus, we give them ours in return.

3. You Trust Each Other

Trust is an essential foundation in any friendship. Otherwise, you are meant to fall apart. It would help if you grew that trust slowly. When you are loyal to each other, then there is nothing that comes between you two. You need to develop that trust slowly. When you are dedicated to each other, then there is nothing that comes between you two. Honesty is a must when it comes to building your trust with each other. If even one of you is lying about anything, then that friendship fails. Even if they didn't keep their promise, you can't trust them.

4. They Hype You Up

They won't fall back on complimenting you when you look your best. But a friend won't hesitate to confront you if you don't look good. That is what we like about them, and they won't make you look bad in front of others. They will make sure you know you are worth it. They will make you work for what you deserve. Friends will always try to hype you up and will accolade you. They know what you like and don't, so they shape you like you want to be shaped.

5. You Share Almost Everything

Two friends are always together in spirits. When something noteworthy happens in your life, you always feel the need to share it with someone. That someone will probably be a friend. You tend to share every little detail of any event of your life with them comfortably. They listen to you. And sometimes, they need to be listened to. That's where you come. You listen to them. Even the most intimate secrets are told sometimes. This exchanging of secrets can only be done when you feel safe sharing them with a person. A friend buries your secrets within themselves.

6. Good Memories

Even the most boring party can take a 360 degree turn when you are with your friend. Times like these call for good memories. It would help if you shared loads of good memories. Even when time passes by, a bad day can make an excellent future memory.

Conclusion

It takes a lot of time, care and love to form a strong bond of friendship. We have to give it our best to keep that bond in good condition. Friends are precious to us, and we should make them feel likewise. And with the right person, friendship can last a lifetime.

Chapter 25:

6 Signs You Are Emotionally Unavailable

In times of need, all we want is emotional comfort. The people around us mainly provide it. But the question is, will we support them if the need arises? You might be emotionally unavailable for them when they need you. It is necessary to have some emotional stability to form some strong bonds. If you are emotionally unapproachable, you will have fewer friends than someone you stand mentally tall. It is not harmful to be emotionally unavailable, but you need to change that in the long run. And for that, you need to reflect on yourself first.

It would help if you always were your top priority. While knowing why you are emotionally unapproachable, you need to focus on yourself calmly. Giving respect and talking is not enough for someone to rely on you. You need to support them whenever needed. Talk your mind with them. Be honest with them. But not in a rude way, in a comforting way. So, next time they will come to you for emotional support and comfort. If you are relating to all these things, then here are some signs that confirm it.

1. You Keep People At A Distance

It is usual for an emotionally unavailable person to be seen alone at times. They tend to stay aloof at times; that way, they don't have to be emotionally available. And even if you meet people, you always find it challenging to make a bond with them. You might have a few friends and family members close to you. But you always find meeting new people an emotionally draining activity. You also might like to hang out with people, but opening up is not your forte. If you are emotionally unavailable, then you keep people at a hands distance from you.

2. You Have Insecurities

If you struggle to love yourself, then count it as a sign of emotional stress. People are likely to be unavailable emotionally for others when they are emotionally unavailable for themselves too. We always doubt the people who love us. How can they when I, myself, can't? And this self-hatred eventually results in a distant relationship with your fellow beings. Pampering yourself time by time is essential for every single one of us. It teaches us how one should be taken care of and how to support each other.

3. You Have A Terrible Past Experience

This could be one of the reasons for your unapproachable nature towards people. When you keep some terrible memory or trauma stored inside of you, it's most likely you cannot comfort some other being. It won't seem like something you would do. Because you keep this emotional difference, you become distant and are forced to live with those memories, making things worse. It would help if you talked things out. Either your parents or your friends. Tell them whatever is on your mind, and you will feel light at heart. Nothing can change the past once it's gone, but we can work on the future.

4. You Got Heartbroken

In most cases, people are not born with this nature to be emotionally unavailable. It often comes with heartbreak. If you had a breakup with your partner, that could affect your emotional life significantly. And if it was a long-term relationship, then you got emotionally deprived. But on the plus side, you got single again. Ready to choose from scratch. Instead, you look towards all the negative points of this breakup. Who knows, maybe you'll find someone better.

5. You Are An Introvert

Do you hate going to parties or gatherings? Does meeting with friends sound tiresome? If yes, then surprise, you are an introvert. Social life can be a mess sometimes. Sometimes we prefer a book to a person. That trait of ours makes us emotionally unavailable for others. It is not a bad thing to stay at home on a Friday night, but going out once in a while may be healthy for you. And the easiest way to do that is to make an extrovert friend. Then you won't need to make an effort. Everything will go smoothly.

6. You Hate Asking For Help

Do you feel so independent that you hate asking for help from others? Sometimes when we get support from others, we feel like they did a favor for us. So, instead of asking for help, we prefer to do everything alone, by ourselves. Asking for aid, from superior or inferior, is no big deal. Everyone needs help sometimes.

Conclusion

Being emotionally unavailable doesn't make you a wrong person, but being there for others gives us self-comfort too. It's not all bad to interact with others; instead, it's pretty fun if you try. It will make your life much easier, and you will have a lot of support too.

Chapter 26:

10 Signs You've Outgrown Your Friendship

There is almost no one in this world that doesn't have a friend. Some of us even have ten best friends. It all depends on two factors. First is that you have to pick a type of friend and second one is that you find them in this life. Mostly everyone has. Since childhood, you might have had lots of friends. But, did they stay? We eventually have to leave them behind even if we don't want to. It's important to know when to leave them behind, and here are ten signs that you've outgrown your friendship.

1. You disregard them:

When you've outgrown your friendship with someone, you ignore them. You forget spending time with them. It is unhealthy for a company to disregard each other in any way. So, you naturally drive apart from them. You start to choose different places to hang instead of hanging around with them like you used to.

2. You pretend:

When you are with a friend, all you want is to be yourself. And when you feel like you need to pretend like someone else or like your old self, that's a red flag. You might not fall into each other's expectations of grownups. And it disappoints you both. Compatibility is a key to friendship.

3. Lack of effort:

Friendship has to grow in the right places, and if it doesn't, then it's not meant to work out. When there are no efforts from even one side, then you both will break apart. One-sided friendship is draining and tiring. We might be ghosting them without even noticing, so it is always better to cut them off.

4. You get awkward around each other:

One thing that is the most wondrous about friendship is that you can be comfortable around each other even in silence. If you are finding that peaceful silence awkward, then it's an outgrown friendship. It will only make this friendship a burden to you and them. Getting out of this tricky situation means getting out of your company with them.

5. You have nothing to discuss:

Communication is what makes a friendship stronger. When you got nothing to talk about, then you don't have to talk to them at all. There is always something to talk about, and it only depends on the person we are willing to tell. You need to find a person that you want to listen to you.

6. You both are going different ways:

Life takes everyone on a different path. When you and your friend choose other ways, then it's natural for you to weaken your bond with each other. You both will make new friends according to your phases in life, and that is not such a bad deal. Letting go would be healthy in this situation and for your good.

7. Support is unequal:

Supporting each other is extremely important in friendship. And if you or your friend doesn't have this quality, you are not a good match. Sometimes, in times of need. That's all that one wants. Advice in this situation may seem like disagreeing.

8. You keep secrets:

Sharing your day, feelings, and thoughts with your friends sounds like a regular activity for all of us. But some might not agree. When you start to keep things from each other, then that is your weak spot. That is the time you should realize that they are just there for a tag of friend and not playing the actual part.

9. You don't understand each other anymore:

One of the things that keeps a friendship strong is the compatible understanding between the two of you. And if one of you fails to understand the other one, then you've outgrown your company. It's the aspect that completes you both, and without it, you both are just on loose ends.

10. You don't have any more familiar grounds:

It was the mutual interest in certain things that bought you two close enough to be friends. Eventually, you both will find different things likable. Your friend might hate those things and never tell you. But when you sit together and find nothing to talk about. That is where you have to end this friendship.

Conclusion:

Friends might have a significant impact on our lives, but we have to let them go eventually. You will make lots of friends along the way. Leaving one behind doesn't make you the wrong person. It makes you strong one.

Chapter 27:

10 Signs Your Ex Still Loves You

Breakups are very tough to handle. They shatter your heart and have you questioning all your life choices and decisions. You go through a lot of negative emotions, and these tend to be heightened because of the painful words, actions, broken promises, and broken bonds that you both once shared. Despite all of this, it's never easy to let go and move on from a once-strong relationship. There might still be some fragments left that'll give you the idea that maybe your ex is still not over you. Here are some signs you should see to know if your ex still loves you and wants you back.

1. Following your online activities:

If your ex still hasn't blocked you, instead follows all your updates on social media, it might show that they still have concern for you and would like to reconnect with you. The constant likes, comments, and reactions on your posts is also a way of showing that you're constantly on their mind, and they're still not ready to let you go.

2. Nostalgic conversations

Suppose, by any chance, you converse with your ex, and they constantly try to reminisce about your happy moments together or mention how you both could have avoided ending things like this and should have dealt with issues better. In that case, that means they're regretting the breakup. This is also a way of testing how you would react to such conversations and see if another shot at this relationship is possible.

3. Reaching out from time to time:

Suppose your ex reaches out to you during special holidays and events, like your birthday or a wedding of a mutual or even christmas and halloween. In that case, it could be the perfect excuse for them to get closer to you without exposing much of their feelings. If they text you and ask for your help with something, no matter how small or stupid, they are just making efforts to be around you.

4. Staying a bit longer to talk:

You might be familiar with the feeling of joy that you experience each time you talk to a friend who seems close to you and with whom you love sharing things. No matter how much you've spoken or how late you're getting, you still hang with them for just a few minutes more. If you sense that your ex feels the same about you each time you guys meet or talk, they still have some feelings for you.

5. Showing signs of loneliness:

When your ex constantly seems gloomy and upset and lets the whole world know by posting it on social media, it could signify that they are seeking your attention. If they post sad stuff that's relatable to both of you, chances are they're waiting for you to notice it and reach out to them.

6. Trying to patch things up:

Your ex might finally hold themselves accountable for their actions and mistakes and often talk about what they should have done to save the relationship. They may constantly try to reassure you that they have changed and now they're a better person. If this is a recurring theme, then this is a vital sign they want you back.

7. Showing they miss you:

The most significant sign that your ex wants you back is most probably opening up to you and showing you how much they miss you. They might make you remember the old times and share stuff about how miserable they are without you. It's a clear sign that they still love you.

8. Available for help:

If your ex reaches out and offers you their assistance and is always available whenever you need help, they are still looking out for you. This is a good indication showing that they will always be there for you no matter what, and you can rely on them.

9. Backed up by friends:

If your ex's friends or even your friends reach out to you and say that your ex has changed and they still talk about you a lot, they're making you consider going back with them. Chances are, your ex has made a good image in front of your circle to try and win you back.

10. Still single after a long time:

If a long time has passed since your breakup and your ex still hasn't opened up to the idea of dating, it means they still haven't moved on from you and are still lingering on the hope of getting back together with you.

Conclusion:

If you observe these signs with your ex, consider them carefully to make the right decision for yourself.

Chapter 28:

8 Signs Someone Misses You

Missing someone can be very painful, almost as if there is something incomplete about your life. You think about them all the time, and the more you try not to think of them, the more you end up doing that. You might find your thoughts wandering and can't seem to focus on anything other than them. You may either find comfort in binge eating or constantly go through their stuff. Well, you're not the only one who might be going through this torture. What if someone is experiencing the same stuff but for you? Here are some signs that tell you someone is missing you.

1. They keep track of your social media:

If they haven't unfriended, unfollowed, or blocked you yet, the chances are that they are still keeping track of you. If you find them constantly reacting to your stories, or liking your pictures the minute you put them up, then they're visiting your profile again and again. They have kept their slot open for making a conversation or giving you a hint to try to make conversation with them.

2. Did they find your replacement yet?

For someone ready to move on, it takes a second to find a replacement. If they haven't found one yet, the chances are that they are still reminiscing over you. They're hoping that you'll reconnect and thus, still pine after you. Even if they're hooking up with someone as a rebound, chances are they're doing everything in their power to forget you but are failing miserably.

3. They reach out to you randomly:

Receiving those drunk late-night texts/calls? They're miserable, and all they want to do is talk to you. If they were out there having the time of their life, they wouldn't even remember you let alone bother to text or call you. If they do, it's obviously because you're on their mind and alcohol just gave them a head start to get in touch with you again.

4. Rousing your jealousy so you would notice them:

Have they suddenly started posting a lot about their new life on social media? Chances are they're most certainly trying hard to make you sit up and take notice of them. If they're hanging out with a lot of people that you've never seen or heard of and having a fantastic time, then they're trying to make you jealous.

5. They throw shade at you:

If they're making snide comments or remarks about you or a new partner, they're still clearly hurt and miss you. They might pass a statement on your outfit or your appearance and lash out at you, trying to make you feel as bad as they do. They may also show disapproval of your new date and point out negative things about them. It's clear that they still haven't moved on and clung to that thin thread of hope.

6. They do things to get your attention:

Do they post stuff that points towards you? Or do they write cute love letters or poems mentioning you? This is a pretty obvious sign that they miss you and want to get back in their life. They might also ask your friends about you and crash those uninvited parties because they want to see you. You might also see them around more than usual.

7. They hoard your stuff:

Are they still keeping your shirt/hoodie and making excuses not to give it even when you have asked them a million times? Or are they keeping even the most useless thing that you might have given them years ago? It's probably because they go through this stuff and relive all the old memories associated with them. They're still not ready to give them up and move on.

8. From the horse's mouth:

The most obvious and straightforward sign that someone misses you? They tell you themself! Some people don't like to play games and do unnecessary things to gain your attention or throw hints and clues at you and wait for you to notice them. They tell you straight away that they miss you and they want to do something about it.

Conclusion:

Now that you have all the signs on your plate, it's up to you whether you want to give them a second chance or move on from all of this. The choice is yours!

Chapter 29:

6 Gestures That Make People Feel Loved

"Actions speak louder than words ', this phrase is commonly used around us, but hardly anyone knows the real meaning of this phrase. This phrase tells us something about love and the importance of a person. Our actions define us. These actions affect the people around us, it speaks to them in words, we can't speak in. Loving someone is not just enough. You need to show your love, and sometimes the smallest of gestures can make you feel more loved than ever. Everyone wants to feel loved and cared about, and if you truly love them, then show your love, even if it is through a straightforward small text saying, "I miss you." Here are a few ways to make people feel loved.

1. Write Them Notes

Waking up to a heartwarming note on your bedside tables makes someone's day. So whenever you want to show someone how much you love them, just leave them a letter or card. It doesn't matter if you write a few words, either thanking them or telling them how strong they are. These actions affect people the most. It makes them feel loved and, beyond all, appreciated. It also shows that you care about making them feel happy. This note or card will bring a bright smile to their lovely faces.

2. Take Their Favourite Food

"The way to a person's heart is through the stomach," a saying that is quite famous in some parts of the world. Who doesn't feel happy when they get to eat their favorite food. So whoever this person is that you want to make feel loved, on your way back from work, stop by at their favorite restaurant, buy their favorite dish and surprise them with it. Firstly, they will feel loved knowing that you remembered their favorite word and secondly, the food, of course. Now you know whenever someone's feeling low, bring them their favorite food, it'll take their minds off the stressful thing, and they would feel thankful for you.

3. Remind Them Of Their Importance

As easy as it sounds, expressing love is a tricky thing to do. There have been times when we all love someone but don't express it because we feel shy and as a result, they don't feel loved. As everyone grows up, it is easy to feel alone in this world, so always remind people around you how important they are. Tell people you love them, I love you is just a three-word sentence, but the meaning it holds is more profound than the ocean, so don't hesitate and make your loved ones feel loved.

4. Surprise Them

Everyone has different hobbies, and some people like makeup. Someone prefers football over everything else. As everyone is interested in other things, we often hear them talk about these things. Sometimes they talk about how they want something, but they are either saving up for it or don't have the time. Surprise them with things they have talked about and feel excited about. This makes that person feel loved and cared about. They know that you listen to them, and this quality is something that not everyone has.

5. Listen To Them

As I said before, listening is a quality that people often look at in others. We all need that one person who will listen to us and won't interrupt us when we tell them about our day. People feel grateful when they remember that there is still someone that will listen to them no matter what.

6. Include Them In Things That Matter To You

We talked about their interests but remembered you are important too, don't forget about yourself in the process and don't we all know the person who cares about us will always want to know about our lives and support your decisions. So please include them in things that are important to you, fill them in on the ongoing drama of your life, and inform them about your decisions before you take a step ahead.

<u>Conclusion:</u>

When you make someone feel loved, you feel happy, and so do they. Isn't it amazing how easily, by following these steps, you can make someone feel loved? So don't hesitate. Go ahead and show them your love because life's too short to stay hesitant.

Chapter 30:

5 Signs Someone Only Likes You As A Friend

There's nothing like the feeling of getting friend-zoned by a guy/girl you so desperately wanted to be with. When theoretical physicists started talking about black holes, they were probably referring to the friend zone. You find yourself drooling and crushing hard over them, only to find out that they have never reciprocated those feelings. Spotting the signs that they just want to be friends with you and nothing more is always disappointing. But the sooner you see them, the easier it will be for you to move on.

Sure, it might be a little complex for you at first, as some people tend to be very poor in communicating and can give mixed signals, which might make you confused. It could lead to a bunch of misunderstandings between you two and may also cause you to daydream about them when there isn't anything for you. Here are some subtle signs that they only like you as a friend.

They Never Get Jealous

Overly jealous people can be considered toxic ones, and jealousy isn't always a good thing. But sometimes, in small amounts, it might show that one person does care enough about the other to want them all to themselves. If the person you like never gets jealous when you're flirting with other people, or when others are showing their interest in you, then it means they don't care about your love life and sees you only as a friend who's having fun. On the contrary, if they show some emotion or are affected by you flirting with others, it might mean they're interested in you.

They Are Always Trying To Set You Up With Their Friends

If you're romantically interested in someone, then it's not a great sign if they're your matchmaker all the time. Relationships might start like this only in the movies, while the reality is different. It's improbable that someone would set up a person they like with their friend or their acquaintance. If they're constantly on your nerve asking you to date people or are being your wing person, then it's a sign they consider you only as a friend.

There's No Flirting From Their

If two people are really into each other and spend most of their time together, then it's nearly impossible for them not to flirt, even if it's a little bit. It's always in their subconscious mind to praise and appreciate someone they like. While some people aren't the flirty type, and some are just straight-up awkward or shy, we can always filter out if they're petrified or just downright ignoring us. If they don't flirt with you ever, like in any way, or if your flirty remarks make them uncomfortable and they reject your attempts straight away, then it could mean that they're not interested in you.

They Discuss Their Love Life With You

Most of the time, people wouldn't gush about their romantic lives in front of you if they seem interested in you. It would simply send out the signal that they aren't available to you. They might talk about their ex-lovers to try to make you jealous or talk about people who are into them to try to impress you, but that's an entirely different kettle of fish. While it can be hard to tell the difference, see if he genuinely seeks your love advice or seems overly interested in someone else. That would mean he likes someone else and not you.

They Rarely Text You Or Asks About You

When someone likes you, they tend to find excuses to text you and talk to you all the time. They might start by asking silly questions that they already knew the answer to, or may indulge in deep conversations with you, or direct the subject elsewhere so that they have a chance to talk to you. They might even ask your friends or friends about you and try to find you when you're not around. On the contrary, if they hardly text you or call you or even don't try to communicate with you, then it's a clear sign that they might not be interested in you.

Conclusion

You should try and be clear about your feelings and ask them to do the same since day one, as it could save both of you from confusion and getting mixed signals and fantasizing about something that doesn't even exist in the first place. You cannot make someone love you, no matter how much you wish you could.

Chapter 31:

5 Ways To Reject Someone

Nicely

Rejecting someone can be pretty hard as we never want that to happen to us as well. But leading onto something that you don't wish to will end up getting you both frustrated and confused. So, it is better to be true to yourself and the other person who feels something for you. That one-sided feeling has to come to a stop at some point, and only you can stop that. You don't need to blame yourself, but an apology would be an excellent way to reject someone. It is, no doubt, the most challenging part of dating.

Try to inform them as soon as possible, that way you will not be wasting any of their time. It can be uncomfortable and awkward to you and them, but it is necessary to do it. And we need to be as gentle and kind as possible while rejecting someone. It can be as hard as getting rejected yourself. It would be best if you picture yourself in their place. It would help if you treated them the way exactly as you want to be treated while getting rejected by someone.

1.Be Honest To Them

When you are rejecting someone, you need to avoid small talks as much as possible. It will only waste your time as well as yours. Be as honest as possible for yourself. It would be best if you told them all the valid reasons for their failure. Keep calm the whole time. Try to be straightforward with the person in front of you. There is no point in dragging things out if the income will be the same in the end. Make sure you try not to hurt them and disappoint them. And after all this, you both have your journey to continue.

2. Choose Your Wording Carefully

You both might go your ways after the rejection, but the words you said will stay with them forever. You need to choose your wording very carefully and make sure it sounds right when spoken. The person in front of you deserves an excellent explanation with a few words of encouragement for him to move on from this rejection. Make sure you choose each word respectfully. Appreciate them for confronting you too. Don't sound too sorry for them. And be very clear on what you have to deliver.

3. Do It In Person

The worst rejection you can give anyone is through a message or a phone. Try to go yourself to reject someone. If you are unable to reach the person for talking for any reason, you have to make sure that you keep the conversation on the phone as authentic as possible. Try to go yourself to give them support. Show them that it is hard for you both to sit there. Its common courtesy to make the other person think that this conversation is vital for you. Show up on time and make sure you deliver your message fully.

4. Don't Give False Hope

If you are not interested in someone, a clear, blunt "no" will do. Don't go by the fear of breaking a heart. You will give that person false hope about dating, and you both will end up unhappy about it. It will waste a lot of your time and theirs. They will move on more quickly if you let them go early. You cannot force the feeling into you. And the other person would be thankful too for your honesty which saved you both from something that was never meant to happen. Just let them be and let them recover from you on their own. That will be the best you could do for them.

5. Don't Blame Them

It would help if you accepted the fact that you are going to hurt them no matter what. And the truth is it was never their fault, to begin with. We cannot choose whom we like in our life. When reasoning, give a lot of "I" statements. Don't point out their issues and faults, and it will only make them hurt more. It is always easier to use the "It's not you, it me "approach with the person you are rejecting. They have to bear with the bad news on their own.

Conclusion

We all want that spark in a relationship, and the lack of it can be equally disappointing to you. But if the other person feels that spark, then you have to light it out quickly. They should move on with someone new in their life and you with someone who can give you that same spark you were craving.

CPSIA information can be obtained
at www.ICGtesting.com
Printed in the USA
LVHW050356210122
708836LV00015B/690